MW00719342

HAL'S NAVY

by
Cdr. Harold H. Sacks USN (Ret.)

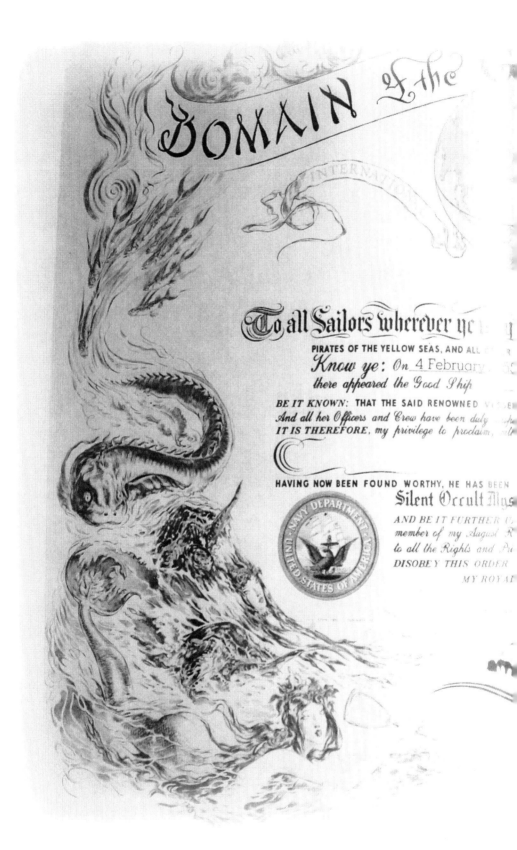

DOMAIN of the

To all Sailors wherever ye

PIRATES OF THE YELLOW SEAS, AND ALL

Know ye : On 4 February
there appeared the Good Ship

BE IT KNOWN: THAT THE SAID RENOWNED
And all her Officers and Crew have been duly
IT IS THEREFORE, my privilege to proclaim,

HAVING NOW BEEN FOUND WORTHY, HE HAS BEEN

Silent Occult Mys

AND BE IT FURTHER
member of my August
to all the Rights and Pu
DISOBEY THIS ORDER
MY ROYAL

HAL'S NAVY

by

Cdr. Harold H. Sacks,
USN (Ret.)

PARKE PRESS
Norfolk

Dedicated to Annabel, my forever shipmate

For more information, contact:
Cdr. Harold H. Sacks, 530 Boissevain Ave., Norfolk, VA 23507
757-622-2003 • dcgrp@mindspring.com

Published by Parke Press, Norfolk, Virginia
Book Design: Marshall Rouse McClure

Library of Congress Cataloging-In-Publication Data:
Available upon request.

Hardback ISBN 978-0-988369-4-4
Softback ISBN 978-0-988369-3-7

Printed in the United States of America

★

TABLE OF CONTENTS

★

AN INTRODUCTION

WHEREAS it is customary to thank those responsible for making this effort possible, the author wishes to thank: First, the People's Republic of North Korea, for invading South Korea in 1950, and then for insisting on repatriation of 80,000 North Korean POWs which President Truman wisely refused, thus precluding a cease-fire in 1951. (Otherwise, I would not have faced a draft into the Army in 1952.) Second, I need to thank my wife, Annabel, for agreeing to a career in the Navy. Third, I am very grateful for those officers who decided I was worth their efforts to mold a half-baked reserve officer into a regular Navy officer on a command track.

What follows is, with one or two exceptions (such as the extended description of Cold War operations in the Black Sea), solely the product of the author's memory, without the benefit of any serious research. Any errors of recall, therefore, after half a century in some instances, are unintentional and one hopes they will be forgiven.

The author realizes that memoirs, by their very nature, are self-serving. He does not apologize for what follows.

★ ★ ★

Coming On Board

IN THE SUMMER OF 1951, with the "Police Action" in Korea heating up and the draft in progress, the likelihood of military service in the army loomed. Taking a break from my graduate studies at Columbia University, I made my way to 346 Broadway in New York City, the Office of Naval Officer Procurement. Ascending the stairs and stopping at the first office, I was greeted by a Marine Sergeant with many hash-marks on his uniform sleeve.

"What are you offering?" I asked.

"College graduate?" he queried.

When I replied affirmatively, he went into his pitch: "Well, sir, all you have to do is take a little multiple-choice test and within 30 days, upon passing the physical exam, you will be sworn in, sent to Officer Candidate School in Quantico, Virginia, and in 120 days commissioned as a Second Lieutenant in the United States Marine Corps. This is strictly a fighting man's commission and you will be ordered to command an infantry platoon in Korea."

Perhaps I can be forgiven for thanking the sergeant, declining that invitation and proceeding to the Navy office. I took the Navy's test (which I fortunately passed) and shortly thereafter reported for the physical examination (again, fortunately passed). Ordinarily that would have put me, at the age of 21, in Class II, Officer Candidate School (OCS), commencing September 1951. However, the Navy was willing to defer my orders to active duty for one year to allow me to complete my graduate work. Thus it was that in September of 1952, one month following marriage to Annabel Glicksman, Officer Candidate Seaman Recruit (E1) Harold Sacks reported for duty in Class  VIII at the Naval Officer Candidate School in Newport, Rhode Island.

Assigned to Company L, Section 4, I saw the first days go by in a blur. Reveille for L Company is at 0530; breakfast at 0600. Marching silently and raggedly to the mess hall, this Jewish boy from the Bronx has his initial introduction to the Navy menu (set in stone by Navy League wives in 1919). My much-loved lox and bagels are replaced by creamed chipped beef on toast (indelicately dubbed "Foreskins on Toast"); what appears to be spaghetti sauce with ground beef on toast (similarly dubbed "S.O.S – Shit on a Shingle"); a gluey bit of white goop called grits; hard-clumped scrambled eggs; runny not-quite-hardboiled eggs; cold Navy beans. Our mess cooks (mainly disciplinary cases from the fleet) take special pleasure in flipping the butter into our coffee. At dinner they flip the butter into the ice cream which lies melting on the hot, stainless steel compartmented trays.) How ironic that I learned to love all of the above dishes and crave them to this day!

Breakfast is not the place to dawdle; it begins at 0600. At 0620: We form up for muster and inspection. 0630: L Company reports to the pistol range. 0800: First Period.

We stagger to the barrack under a two-and-a-half foot stack of books (*Ship Handling, Navigation, Dutton, H.O. 214, Nautical Almanac, Naval Boilers, Naval Engines, Damage Control, Operations, Naval Communications, Weapons, Seamanship, Boatswain's Mate 3/c, ATP-1, ACP 175, Watch Officer's Guide*), protractor, parallel ruler, calipers, three-ring binder, L/L paper, pencils and pens.

We stagger once again to the barrack under a two-and-a-half foot stack of uniforms (undress blues, dress blues,

dress shoes, dungaree trousers and chambray shirts [work uniform], "boondock" high shoes, skivvies [underwear], white hat, flat hat, watch cap, pea coat, foul weather jacket, poncho, sweater, shaving kit, shoeshine kit, sewing kit and marker pen). Our dungarees are not sized to length; thus, the sewing kit. We are expected to measure the length, cut them to size and sew up the hems. Thankfully, some of our sectionmates come from the fleet and provide technical support. I learned my lessons well and have sewn my own buttons for over half a century.

CHIEF PETTY OFFICERS (CPOs) in the Navy are not saluted by the lower grades, except at OCS. Officer Candidates salute everyone and, virtually, every thing. Chief

Machinist's Mate John V. Sullivan is our Company Chief. "Sully" served in battleships and destroyers in WWII. He tries very hard to be a tough drill sergeant but turns out to be more of a mother hen. That is, with the exception of the first month – a kind of a "hell month," both academically and militarily. The entire staff at OCS was seemingly dedicated to applying as much pressure as possible to weed out the weakest candidates during the first few weeks. And they succeed. More than a few in my section last just one month. The penalty for failure is orders to boot camp prior to joining the fleet as a seaman.

Chief Sullivan personally assigns the barrack cleaning stations. Mine is the large urinal in the second deck head. The urinal is about four feet wide and designed to be used by several men at one time, and it is my job to give it a light cleaning every day and a thorough preparation for inspection on Friday. The Chief makes it clear when he says, "Sacks, this is your cleaning station. I expect it to be the cleanest urinal in the United States Navy. Is that understood?" "Aye Aye! Chief,"[1] I reply. The first Friday inspection is a disaster. "Soap scum on the edges! Verdigris on the piping! This week you get a warning. Next week, no weekend pass. Is that understood?" "Aye Aye! Chief." One of the fleet men gave me an old toothbrush and tells me to swipe some powdered lemonade from the galley to use on the pipes. It works! The acid takes off all the crud and the urinal sparkles. My first success in the Navy!

Success is very important because it is linked to weekend liberty, such as it is. Personnel inspection is at 0900 Saturday mornings. Friday night we spit-shine our dress shoes and shape

---

[1] A word here on the difference between "Yes, Sir" and "Aye Aye, Sir." "Aye Aye" is unique to the Navy. "Yes, Sir" is an acknowledgement that the order has been received. "Aye Aye" is an acknowledgement that the order is received, is *understood* and will be carried out.

our inspection white hat into the correct fleet look. If we pass inspection (and somehow I always manage), liberty commences at 1000 Saturday. Then the race is on to Providence, Rhode Island, to catch the N.Y. Central's 1200 train to Grand Central Station, arriving about 1600. Newly married and without a home of our own, Annabel and I enjoy an overnight "long weekend" either in her parents' or my parents' home. Sunday I catch a 1300 train back to Providence in order to check in no later than 1900 to prepare for Monday quizzes.

> *"In writing this manual, full consideration was given the midshipmen's excellent background in chemistry, physics, fluid mechanics and thermo-dynamics."*
> Introduction, Combustion Engines Manual

THUS BEGAN THE CURRICULUM at OCS. The perceptive saw the handwriting on the wall. A master's degree in English Literature has a certain undeniable aura in a social or academic setting, but hardly provides the equipment to cope with metacentric heights and dynamic stability. The Naval Academy texts were undecipherable. I was plunged into a nightmarish electro-mechanical world – breech-blocks, amplidynes and electrolytes played tag with each other in an esoteric manner, sidereal hour angles tossed direction to the winds and were seen in public with diurnal circles. I managed to control my dismay and grope through, even when faced with a pamphlet purporting to be a review of two semesters of trigonometry marked, "Reading Time: 15 minutes."[2]

Seamanship was easy meat. We learned to do arithmetically what a gyrocompass did automatically, to adjust for magnetic

[2] The author's memory was aided by referring to our class yearbook, **The Sea Chest**, dated December 1952, for which he was one of the principal writers.

deviation and geo-
graphic variance. Age-
old mnemonics helped
memorization: "Can
Dead Men Vote Twice,"
or reversed, "True
Virgins Make Dull
Company." We learned
about can buoys (black)
and nun buoys (red)
and that entering port
the red buoys were to
starboard, "Right Red
Returning," and even
numbers, "Even Red
Nuns Have Odd Black
Cans". We memorized
the Rules of the Road,
and the meaning of
running lights: "Red
over White – Fishing
at Night"; "White over
Red – Pilot Ahead";
"Red over Red – (Out
of Command) – Captain
is Dead."

After-dinner study hall

But the most absorbing were the courses in maneuvering
and tactics. The pending introduction to the fleet of two new
publications to govern operations at sea and visual signaling gave
us a chance to learn something even before shipboard officers
did. ATP-1 (Allied Tactical Publication-1) and ACP-175 (Allied
Communication Publication) were to replace virtually all the
standard publications of their type in the Navy as we geared

up to operate jointly with NATO forces. Even the old Navy phonetic lettering (Able, Baker, Charlie, Dog, Easy...) was to be replaced by a new set more easily pronounced and understood by non-English speaking Naval forces: Alpha, Bravo, Charlie, Delta, Echo.... (In my next chapter this will prove to have some relevance.)

Entering the last month of OCS, with graduation set for December 1952, two significant events are recalled. First, we were fitted for and ordered our officer's uniforms: one set service dress blue; one service dress khaki; one dress white; one cap, with officer's insignia and blue, khaki, and white covers; gray and white gloves; various collar bars and shoulder boards.

Second, and most memorably, we filled out our duty preference forms. Choices ranged from Communications Watch Officer, Wake Island, or Paris, to the full spectrum of shipboard and shore-based assignments. With a total lack of knowledge (in my Bronx upbringing) regarding the range of naval billets, I cleverly consulted with my section-mates and learned that assignment to shipboard duty would involve *class standing*. (I never seemed to have the inside scoop.) Combatant ship assignments were for those in the top half of the class and small combatants were for those in the top one-third. The thought of being a lowly Ensign on a battleship with 2,000 men, or on an aircraft carrier with 5,000 men seemed unappealing. I recalled something I had read by John Steinbeck:

> *A destroyer is a lovely ship, probably the nicest fighting ship of all. Battleships are a little like steel cities or great factories of destruction. Aircraft carriers are floating flying fields. Even cruisers are big pieces of machinery, but a destroyer is all boat. In the beautiful clean lines of her, in her speed and roughness, in her curious gallantry, she is completely a ship in the old sense.*

So I asked for duty aboard a small combatant (destroyer, destroyer escort, or mine craft) and specifically requested the Atlantic Fleet, mindful of the fact that Korea was somewhere in the west Pacific Ocean. I was thrilled to be assigned to a Norfolk, Virginia, destroyer, USS *Owen* (DD 536). However, I was less thrilled to learn that three days after I reported aboard it was departing for Korea. I had somehow overlooked the Panama Canal.

But that was some weeks away. In the meantime, we made plans to invite wives and sweethearts up for graduation and engaged Tex Beneke and the Glenn Miller Orchestra to play for our graduation ball. My last thoughts of OCS include: paying Chief Sullivan $1 for the first salute from an enlisted man; thanking Lt. Hal Curry, our Company Officer, for his guidance; Dean Martin singing the Number 1 hit, "Memories Are Made of This;" and heading home with Annabel for 10 days leave before reporting to my first ship for duty.

CHAPTER TWO

★ ★ ★

The Early Years at Sea
PART 1

**USS *Owen* (DD 536) Deployment to Korea,
January–August 1953**

*"No ship on the oceans of the world
demands as much of her crew as the destroyer."*

THE FRENETIC BRIEF LEAVE between commissioning and departure to my first duty station thankfully came to an end. I say "thankfully" because the impending eight-month deployment was almost un-bearable to contemplate for newlyweds like us. My parents drove me to the airport in early January 1953 to board the (now defunct) National Airlines flight to Norfolk, Virginia and accompanied me onto the tarmac. (Yes, in those days visitors could escort passengers right up to the gangway leading to the aircraft. There were no jet ways; in fact there were no jets). A tearful hug and Mom handed me a copy of Herman Wouk's best-seller, *The Caine Mutiny*. It couldn't have been more appropriate. I had just finished my graduate work at Columbia and the novel is heard through the voice of a newly minted ensign, a graduate of Columbia. I read the book during my limited spare time enroute Panama from Norfolk and identified very strongly with Ensign Keith's tribulations. However, our skipper, Commander Oscar

"Red" Dreyer, in no fashion resembled Keith's CO – although we did have our version of the "strawberry incident". But I get ahead of myself.

The taxi from the airport in Norfolk dropped me at the Convoy-Escort Piers (CE Piers) and the Marine sentry phoned the ship for a two-man working party. They arrived in a pick-up truck, hoisted my suitcase and sea bag aboard and took me to the ship, nested outboard of three other destroyers. I saluted everything that moved, and received

Annabel and Hal on their wedding day, August 12, 1952

permission to board the USS *Owen* (DD 536). To say that I was nervous and excited doesn't begin to describe my feelings. Escorted below to "Officers' Country" I was introduced to the Command Duty Officer, Lt. Joe Saraceno, a World War II naval reservist called back to duty. He was to be a mentor and friend throughout the cruise, despite the differences in our age and rank.

THE USS *OWEN* (DD 536), named after Commander Elias K. Owen who commanded the ironclad *Louisville* in the Mississippi Squadron from 1862-64, was launched at the Bethlehem Steel Company, San Francisco, California, commissioned in 1943 and received a baptism of fire as a member of the Fifth Fleet. She participated in the capture of the Marshall Islands and fought in battles to take Palau, Hollandia, and Truk. She was part of the task force involved in the capture, occupation and defense of the Marianas and joined in the Battle of the Philippine Sea on June 30, 1944, during which operation she rescued eight downed pilots. *Owen* then joined Admiral Halsey's Third Fleet, shared in the first strikes on the Philippines, fought in the Battle of Leyte Gulf, helping to sink a Japanese heavy cruiser. Toward the end of the war she was in the thick of the fight against Japanese Kamikaze pilots before heading for home in June of 1945, having earned 11 battle stars. Decommissioned in 1947, *Owen* sat idly until 1951, when she was recommissioned, overhauled and transferred to the Atlantic Fleet. On January 7, 1953 she steamed out of Norfolk for duty in Korean waters. We couldn't foresee what would be asked of us in the coming months, but I know I was not the only person aboard who hoped we would do nothing to discredit the proud record of the men who sailed and fought in *Owen* during World War II.

Cdr. Oscar F. "Red" Dreyer was our Commanding Officer and it was immediately apparent that he was not on the best of terms with the senior reserve lieutenants who had been called back to active duty. They were mostly angry to have been recalled and appeared to resent the authority of the Captain. Part of the problem may have been his youth. Dreyer was only 36, the same age as the reserve lieutenants, had a distinguished war career and *Owen* was his third destroyer command, his first being at age 29. In retrospect he may have been a bit autocratic although for some reason he was always very even tempered, even kind to me. He went on to command the cruiser USS *Little Rock* (CL92) and retired as a Captain.

Our Executive Officer was Lcdr. John Townley Law, who was destined to have a fine career with heavy emphasis on staff work. As was the case with the skipper, the XO found it difficult to gain the respect of *Owen*'s senior lieutenants. Whatever the glitch, it was the XO who was called to the bridge by the Captain. Dreyer would glare at him with his bushy red eyebrows in a frightening frown and Law would generally say, "No problem, Captain, no problem. I have it under control."

ASSIGNED INITIALLY to standing watches in the forward engine room (a maze of valves, pipes, pumps and other auxiliary equipment, accompanied by the constant roar of powerful blowers abetting slightly the enervating high temperatures), I struggled to trace the flow of energy that propelled the ship and provided heat and light for the maintenance of ship and crew. My principal accomplishment during these watches was learning how to descend and ascend a vertical ladder with a cup of coffee in each hand. We smoked incessantly, the forced air blowers burning through the cigarettes in less than two minutes. Breaks were taken on the main deck, port side, where a large deck winch was located. I would sit there cooling off, sometimes conversing with Chief Machinists Mate (MMC) Edwards, who sympathized with my lack of engineering aptitude. At other times I just sat there mesmerized by the seascape, and the beauty of the bioluminescence kicked up by the speeding ship.

Transiting the Panama Canal was both an education and an entertainment. Opened in 1914 after almost forty years of farce and failure, the canal is a marvel of engineering and design, operating virtually perpetually ever since. Accustomed to washing down the ship with salt water, the crew had a good time shifting to fresh water in Gatun Lake, with at least as much water getting on themselves as on the ship.

Enroute San Diego the squadron engaged in tactical drills, dubbed "tictacs" by the crew. As the junior ensign (always called "George") my role on the bridge was to stay as far in the background and remain as inconspicuous as possible. But the bridge was in utter chaos as the Captain, senior officers (there were five WW II-era lieutenants recalled for duty), and signalmen grappled with the just issued tactical publications. The old U.S. Fleet (USF) manuals had just been replaced by Allied Tactical Publication One (ATP-1) and Allied Communication Publications, brought about by the creation of NATO, and the squadron was utilizing them for the first time.

It was a circus. As the Commodore signaled "prepare to reorient the screen by Method Rum," the Captain shouted, "Which way do we turn? Which way do we turn?" And the Officer of the Deck (OOD) called down to the Combat Information Center (CIC), "Combat! Which way do we turn and what course do we come to?" Others on the bridge buried their heads in the publications, vainly attempting to make sense of it all. Thus, when the George ensign had the temerity to offer the correct answer, he was summarily glared upon and his advice ignored. But after three or four equally tumultuous evolutions, with the George ensign (having only recently studied these new publications in OCS), offering the correct answer, grudging respect was given and, for the good of the United States Navy and the *Owen's* engineering department, Ensign Sacks was reassigned to deck watches under Lt. Saraceno.

Life at sea took on a rhythm established during WWII. Dawn and Dusk Alerts, during which the ship went to General Quarters, were held almost every day in preparation for entering the combat zone. These turned out to be unnecessary precautions since neither the North Koreans nor Soviet aircraft ever attacked the Seventh Fleet ships. My GQ station was "Sky 1," in charge of two quad 40mm gun mounts. Sky 1 was located between the two smokestacks and I was practically knocked out by the choking stack gases. If the engineers let loose a puff of black smoke, I would be covered with a liberal coating of soot. Sixty years later, during a visit to the United States Navy Memorial in Washington, D.C., I was pleased to find a model of the USS *Owen* in the "Presidents Room," and there, just aft of the number-one stack was my perch, overlooking the quad 40s. For a moment I could swear I smelled those fumes again.

We stood regular watches, four hours on/eight hours off, between which we attended to our division officer duties:

supervision of cleaning; maintenance; and training. Junior officers were required to perform a day's work each month in navigation, commencing with star sights at dawn, noon sun lines, and concluding with evening star sights at dusk, reporting the ship's position at 0800, 1200 and 2000. We normally ate meals at the second sitting, unless part of the oncoming watch. Sleep was squeezed in whenever possible, although as the junior officer in a two man stateroom now occupied by three men, my bunk was a simple flat spring and an inch-and-and-half mattress slung between the upper and lower bunks. It was so narrow that during the night, if I wanted to turn over, I had to slide out part

Kwan Woogon, Korean Naval Academy Graduate, my roommate for 3 months while I was an engineering trainee

way, turn over and then slide back in. The bunk was supported by chains which came in handy to wrap my arm around in rough weather, preventing my being tossed to the deck.

Our trans-Pacific cruise featured a brief stop at Pearl Harbor which enabled us to visit Honolulu and the fabled Waikiki Beach. We refueled at Wake Island, home of the gooney birds, before arriving at Sasebo, Japan on February 12. Most memorable were the freezing deck watches during our frequently stormy transit. One officer had to be on the open bridge at all times; the other could seek shelter in the pilot house. When the bow dug in and green water swamped the conning station I was soaked; salt water caused neck rashes. Wet foul weather gear never fully dried before it was time to re-don them for the next watch. Many officers were seasick; I never suffered too much and was able to eat and retain each meal. One of my roommates, Dick Andrews, a Kings Point Maritime Academy graduate, was apparently immune to *mal de mer*; the other, Ensign Dick Watson, was seasick so often he earned the nickname "Barf," and was Barf Watson for the rest of the deployment.

All the time I was learning, learning, learning. I learned how to get a motor whale boat lowered; how to drop and weigh anchor; how to calibrate a five-inch dual-purpose gun; how to prepare a torpedo for firing; how to keep station in formation; how to control the main battery during a shore fire assignment; how to spot our fire accurately to the target from a shore position; how to stand a quarterdeck watch in port – all without getting any young sailors hurt. I already had a Masters Degree; this was a doctoral program in progress.

I can summarize our cruise as follows:

1/7-2/12/53 – Departed Norfolk, Virginia enroute Sasebo Japan, via Panama Canal, San Diego, Pearl Harbor, and Midway Island. Crossed the International date line 2/4/53.

2/16-3/7/53 – Operated with the Fast Carrier Task Force in Korean Waters (TF 77).

3/21-4/3/53 – Operated with the Blockade and Escort Force (TF 95) CO USS *Owen* (DD536). Assumed duties as Commander Yang Do Defense and Blockade Unit (CTU 95.2.2). 3/23/53 *Owen* taken under fire by enemy shore batteries. Yang Do Island was defended by a company of Korean marines and a platoon of U.S. Marines. They needed our dunnage to build a school and some empty 5" powder cans for urinals. In exchange they gave us bushels of giant crabs which we steamed and ate in various forms including roast turkey stuffed with crabmeat.

4/5-4/12/53 – Visited the city of Yokosuka, Japan.

4/23-5/8/53 – CO *Owen* relieved as CTU 95.2.2. *Owen* proceeded to Wonsan Harbor, North Korea. *Owen* was taken under fire nine times by enemy shore batteries on 23, 24, 25, 26,

27, 28, 30 April and May 2, 3, receiving a direct hit and many near misses on May 2.

5/8-5/15/53 – *Owen* returned to Yang Do Defense and Blockade duty.

5/15-5/16/53 – *Owen* operated with TF 77 (Fast Carrier Group).

5/17-5/28/53 – Upkeep at Sasebo, Japan.

5/29/6/24/53 – Operated with TF 77.

OPERATING WITH THE FAST carriers was primarily a station-keeping task. As a carrier signaled a turn into the wind to land and launch aircraft, we "small boys" (a denigrating term used by "airdales") had to adjust ourselves to their vastly larger turning radius and radial acceleration. Somehow I developed a real knack for this and was given the chance to conn the ship for such evolutions. I think it was the thrill of taking the conn that

A lighter moment on the bridge

overwhelmed me and made me first think of possibly making a career of the Navy.

During our last period of operations with the carriers, I was conning the ship during a particularly complex maneuver: I was to reverse course and pass the carrier fairly close aboard going in the opposite direction with a relative speed of 54 knots (about 60 miles per hour) and then come to the new course just as the carrier turned to it, reducing speed and ending up right on station. Lt. Saraceno gave me a "well done," and I overheard the captain comment to our commodore, Capt Dale Mayberry, "It looks like we have another qualified Officer of the Deck."

HARKING BACK TO THE famous "strawberry" incident in Herman Wouk's *The Caine Mutiny*, we had a similar incident aboard *Owen*. A rare treat for officers and crew was strawberry shortcake, made with frozen strawberries and a kind of canned ersatz whipped cream. Leftovers were placed in the wardroom refrigerator but were quickly consumed by the junior officers. The skipper came down from the bridge during a quiet evening watch to get seconds on the strawberries. Finding them gone he went into a rage, summoned the XO who shakily offered, "no problem, Captain, no problem, we'll break out some more in the morning." The Captain was not mollified but the rest of us thought the whole incident was hilariously reminiscent.

Relieved of her duties, the ship headed for liberty and upkeep in Yokosuka, Japan. During our passage to Yokosuka via the Shimonoseki Straits, I was standing the midwatch (midnight–0400) under Lt. Ferguson. We were deluged with radar contacts on hundreds of Japanese fishing boats that delighted in coming close aboard and cutting across our bow. (It seems they believed our bow would cut the devil off their tail.) Lt. Ferguson called to the captain and said he didn't feel qualified to conn the ship under these circumstances.

First Row: LT. J. F. Saraceno, LT. A. T. Sprauge, CDR. O. F. Dreyer, LT. CDR. J. T. Law, LT. R. Ferguson.
Second Row: ENS. R. M. Andrews, LT jg E. H. Curriden, ENS. J. Marklesin, ENS. J. Alspaugh, LT. jg F. O. Stroup, ENS. H. Sacks, ENS. R. A. Watson.
Third Row: ENS. H. R. Sobel, ENS. R. H. Watson, LT. jg G. B. Palmer, LT. jg N. W. Ingraham, LT. jg J. C. Dennis, ENS. H. F. Ikeler.

Wardroom Officers of the USS *Owen*

The captain turned to me and asked if I was ready to relieve the OOD? I replied, "Yes, sir!" "Ensign Sacks has the deck and the conn," shouted the captain. "Aye, Aye!" responded the bridge watch standers. Then the captain whispered to me, "Steer your course. Don't worry about the fishing boats. They will be watching you and will avoid you. But if by chance you hit one of them, for God's sake don't stop – just keep going."

Fifteen years later, as captain of my own destroyer proceeding to Yokosuka up the same straits, my favorite ensign, Bob Patton, also George for the cruise, had the conn. He began to sweat over the myriad of fishing boats. I leaned over and whispered the same advice my captain had given me fifteen years earlier. Patton made it through the watch and went on to be commanding officer of a guided missile cruiser.

THE MOST SIGNIFICANT combat experiences we had were during our assignment in Wonsan Harbor, a principal rail depot and shipping port of North Korea. Our assignment there was two-fold: first, blockade of the port of Wonsan and second, defense of the YoDo Island headquarters of the U.S. Marine Detachment, some of whom were deployed as spotters on smaller islands in the harbor. YoDo had an airstrip vital for search and rescue operations and for supply and replenishment as well as effectively blockading the harbor and preventing shipping from entering or leaving. Lt. (jg) Girard (Jerry) Palmer, our Communications Officer, who performed liaison duties on YoDo, described the situation well:

> *"The action reports from Wonsan were not encouraging… with U.S. ships being hit on a regular basis. The North Koreans controlled the mountainous mainland, and the U.S. Navy had the water and the islands."*

Palmer recalls the briefing we received from a grim-faced Capt. Mayberry, Division Commodore:

> *"…the enemy guns are accurate and well served. And we may be hit. They've had 2½ years of banging away at ships in this harbor and they're getting the range. Gentlemen, this is a very hostile place…the mine sweepers have done well keeping the channels clear…nonetheless, we have to worry about mines, which can be floated out of the inlets at night….the islands have to be held at all costs, and we are the means to that end."*

ON THREE OCCASIONS, Joe Saraceno and I had the deck during what came to be called the "cocktail hour," right around 1700, when the shore batteries opened fire on *Owen*. They apparently didn't have much radar, but had registered some of their guns on specific coordinates in the harbor and opened fire as the ship approached those locations in its patrol. Our skipper "Red" Dreyer would take the conn; Joe would man the starboard wing of the bridge and I the port, calling out the number and location of the close aboard splashes. We would order up smoke and get the heck out of there while Gun Boss, Lt. (jg) "Doc" Watson would return fire with the two Condition Three mounts. After one such "cocktail party," Joe found the deck around the starboard pelorus littered with foot-long shards of shrapnel from a near miss, miraculously causing Joe nothing more than a tear in his foul weather coat. (Subsequent analysis revealed that the shrapnel was from ammunition manufactured in the United States, much of it of pre-WWII vintage which may explain why the round that hit *Owen* was a dud.)

The squadron doctor, Lt. Carter, found plenty to keep him busy on board. On two occasions the ship lay to while wounded ROK (Republic of Korea) marines were stretchered aboard. They were set down on the main deck, starboard side, just abaft the break where Carter and the Korean doctor who accompanied them performed a hasty triage resulting in the least seriously wounded lying out there all night. They were clearly terrified of what awaited them in surgery.

The wardroom had been converted to an operating theater and several of us were pressed into service as OR attendants. Shrapnel wounds were treated, limbs were amputated, and in one case an eye removed. We were struck by the fact that in all cases where abdominal wounds were presented there were parasitic worms. The Korean doctor shrugged his shoulders and suggested that everyone had them and we were not to be too concerned.

As aforementioned, the presence of a U.S. destroyer in the harbor was primarily to keep our marine forces from being overrun by North Korean forces ashore. The spotters were there to monitor truck convoys and other traffic in and out of Wonsan, calling in air strikes from Task Force 77 when the traffic density

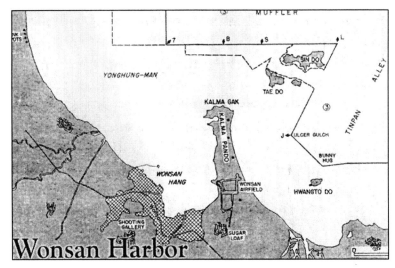

Wonsan Harbor

presented a worthwhile target.

Three days before the *Owen* was hit, the spotter group on Tae Do Island (1 mile from Kalma Gak) took a hit which damaged the slit opening to their bunker and injured some of their personnel. As junior ensign in the Gunnery Department and arguably the most expendable, I received TAD (temporary additional duty) orders to proceed to Tae Do Island with three radiomen strikers and report to the Island Commander for duty as a SFCP (Shore Fire Control Party). In true Hollywood fashion, my roommate and "Bull" (senior) Ensign, Dick Andrews, the Kings Point graduate who went on to become Chief Pilot in the Panama Canal, offered to take my place since I was a newlywed. I, however, was not about to miss what promised to be the adventure of a lifetime.

Our preparations were minimal, helmets and flak vests, 45 caliber automatics, M-1 carbines, portable transceivers and large square batteries. Our chief "stew burner," CSC (Commissaryman Chief) Quartermus, handed us several cases of food, consisting of huge salamis and bolognas ("horse----" in bluejacket parlance), condiments, and many, many loaves of ship-baked bread. *Owen* came to a stop, made a lee for us and our SFCP descended the Jacob's ladder into an LCVP (Landing Craft–Vehicle–Personnel), the famous Higgins Boat of WWII. Our destination: Tae Do Island, located about 1 mile off the Kalma Pando Peninsula, protecting the seaward approaches to the Wonsan airfield. We passed safely through a fusillade of small arms fire, landing on the protected side of the island and were greeted by members of the ROK Marine platoon supporting the U.S. Marine detachment. Their assistance in carrying some of our gear up the 200 meter steep hill to the spotters' bunker was greatly appreciated. Our SFCP's sea legs were great, but our hill climbing legs left much to be desired. "What did you bring to eat, Navy?" shouted First Lieutenant Burke, USMC.

"Horse----, sir!" I replied,

"What? I ought to throw you off my island!"

"But we have five cases of fresh bread, sir," I wheezed.

"All right! Now you're talking," said the Island Commander as he led us into an L-shaped concrete bunker built by the Japanese during WW II. There, to my astonishment, was a huge, gleaming white refrigerator, powered by kerosene, filled with steaks and beer. Burke broke into a big smile, shook my hand and acknowledged that he was mighty glad for the relief and would trade steaks and beer for fresh bread which he hadn't tasted in months.

IN THE NEXT FOUR DAYS my PhD seminar in spotting and survival was to take place.

Our daily routine included breakfast, which commenced at 0600 and concluded at 1000. The shell hit of the previous day had destroyed the cook-stove. Our ROK marine orderly had only a small pot-bellied stove to cook on and, therefore, could make only one hotcake at a time along with a piece of slab bacon.

With ten officers and men in the bunker, it took four hours to feed everyone. On completion, the orderly immediately began preparing lunch.

Tae Do and our neighboring spotters on Hwangto Do also enjoyed a daily "cocktail hour," as North Korean shore batteries lobbed a few shells our way, and annoyingly regaled us with a tattoo of small arms and machine gun fire. With their binoculars they could observe our departure from the bunker to attend to personal needs in the latrine, thirty meters from the bunker. They must have enjoyed a good laugh as they waited until one got "settled", then opened fire. We were protected by a ridgeline, but had insufficient *savoir faire* to remain in the latrine. We must have presented a comical sight scuttling back to the bunker, while hastily pulling up our trousers.

On a more serious note, on day three I and my radiomen were horrified to receive the following message from *Owen*:

"Easy 26 Charlie, this is Drumstick, over."

"26 Charlie roger, over," I replied.

"Hal, is that you? – this is Ike (Ensign Harold Ikeler, CIC Officer), we've been hit and are leaving the harbor. Our ETR is unknown. Keep your f---- head down."

Even the intrepid Marine, Lt. Burke, was concerned now

USS *Owen* (DD 536), completion photo, 8 October 1943

that our principal protector had left us. We spent a very uneasy night, trying not to think of our vulnerability to being overrun. *Owen*'s speedy return to Wonsan Harbor the next day, after they welded a steel plate over the hole in her bow, was announced to cheers on the spotters' net and the Island Commander ordered a round of beers in celebration. A day later I was detached from TAD and transferred by LCVP to *Owen*. No sailor was ever more grateful to report his return aboard.

Radio Moscow, however, reported the *sinking* of the USS *Owen* in Wonsan Harbor. The *New York Times* dutifully reported this and in short order the Bureau of Naval Personnel was besieged by queries from worried dependents. A frantic message from the Chief of Naval Operations inquiring as to our wellbeing resulted in our sending assurances that the ship was afloat and that there had been no casualties.

Welcomed into Yokosuka by two great *Iowa*-class battleships rendering honors to our beat-up WWII destroyer, we were proud to receive the following commendation: "Commander Task Group 95.2 greatly admires conduct of gallant company of ship under intense enemy fire in Wonsan Harbor and is impressed with rapid ship's force repairs and determination to remain on the job."

AMIDST THE RIGORS of shipboard life at sea we learned to enjoy the brief interludes in port.

Sasebo, Japan, for example, had been a major base for the Japanese Navy during WWII, and suffered terrible destruction from allied bombers. By 1953 it had recovered somewhat, yet still displayed many scars. The Japanese had by no means become prosperous; thus, the dollar had huge purchasing power.

There were no real dry cleaning facilities; clothes sent to be cleaned came back smelling as though they had been rinsed in gasoline, hung out to dry, and pressed. But sometimes we had no choice. For example, a clumsy boat crew member dragged a greasy hawser across my service dress khaki uniform, leaving a series of black hash marks across blouse and trousers. When the small Japanese "bumboat" that picked up soiled clothing came alongside while we were anchored in Sasebo, I sent the uniform to be cleaned. Unfortunately, we were ordered to get underway for the gun line several days ahead of schedule and *Owen* sailed before my uniform was returned. I never expected to see it again.

Thirty-five days later, when we steamed into Yokosuka harbor and dropped the hook at the fleet anchorage, a bumboat came alongside and delivered a package to "Ensign Socko." It was my uniform! The young entrepreneur who ran the dry cleaning business in Sasebo had shipped it by train to his cousin who ran the same kind of business in Yokosuka. How all the business people seemed to know the classified movements of our ship was a mystery, but in every port, stores ordered by our supply officer were awaiting us when we arrived. Fifteen years later there was a postscript to this story (*see Chapter 13*).

After one more tour on the gun line, *Owen* left for home the very day the cease-fire went into effect. We were greeted as heroes in port after port as we headed east to complete our "round the world journey", returning via Suez and the Mediterranean Sea.

6/26-7/22/53 – Departed Sasebo enroute Norfolk, Virginia
  Owen visited the following ports enroute:

Manila, Philippine Islands	Athens, Greece
Singapore, British CC	Genoa, Italy
Crossed Equator 7/9/53	Cannes, France
Colombo, Ceylon	Algiers, Algeria
Aden, Aden	Gibraltar, Spain
Suez Canal	Norfolk, Virginia
Port Said, Egypt	

From Panama City and Honolulu to Tokyo, Singapore and Athens, each port of call was an adventure for a young man from New York who had never been overseas.

On our arrival in Norfolk, the wives were waiting on the pier, and I and my Annabel Lee had a tearful but joyous reunion. Annabel, who had never flown before, nor really gone anywhere, somehow made it to Norfolk and rendezvoused with the Wardroom wives.

Wardroom Officers of the USS *Owen* – 35 years later

CHAPTER THREE

★ ★ ★

The Early Years at Sea
PART 2

FOLLOWING OUR RETURN from Korea, the USS *Owen* and crew enjoyed a much-needed period of leave and upkeep, followed by training in the Virginia Capes operating areas. It was an "out to sea on Mondays, back to port on Fridays" routine. Our Skipper was relieved by Cdr Les Hubbell, who went on to flag rank and some renown in the Navy as the author of the "Hubbell

USS *Owen* (DD 536)

Plan", a revolutionary pay and promotion concept. The XO we had sailed with to Korea, Lcdr John Townley Law, who also went on to a splendid career including service as Chief of Staff to the Atlantic Fleet Destroyer Commander, had been relieved by "Mustang" Lt. (soon to be Lt. Comdr.) Joseph Boriotti. Joe was colorful, direct, and a fine mentor. "Mustang" was a term given to officers who came to their commission via service as an enlisted sailor. (Some years later I had the pleasure of instructing aboard a destroyer escort Joe Boriotti commanded while it was in refresher training in Guantánamo Bay, Cuba.)

My Pet – 5" Gun mount #51

A TYPICAL EXERCISE with an atypical outcome was the practice torpedo shoot. Ensign Don Lawrence, a Naval Academy graduate, was the torpedo officer. Joe Boriotti therefore dubbed him "Fish" Lawrence. Exercise torpedoes were 21-inch steam driven anti-ship torpedoes, long since abandoned in the missile age surface navy. The World War II history books are filled with stories of fast destroyers threading their way through punishing salvos from heavy ships in order to fire a spread of torpedoes.

We were supposed to fire two "fish" from a five-tube mount, numbers one and five, representing a full spread. Of course, we were using exercise torpedoes designed to float after their run so that they could be recovered. Just prior to the shoot, the men reported a problem with the firing circuit. However, the Captain decided that we would proceed and that the Officer of the Deck (OOD) would parallel the fire order using the firing keys located

The "Lost Torpedo"

on the bridge. The problem with the firing circuit, as we learned too late, was that the circuit was reversed on the mount. Thus, when "Fire one" was heard and pressed, number five would fire. The result was calamitous. "Fire one!" the Captain ordered. The mount captain pressed one and number five left the mount. Simultaneously, the OOD pressed the switch for number one and number one left the mount. The two torpedoes, fired at the same time, "kissed" and plunged to the bottom of the ocean – never to be seen again. "Fish" Lawrence spent the next several weeks filling out his "lost torpedo" report.

IN SEPTEMBER 1953 I was ordered to Key West Florida for eight weeks of Anti-Submarine Warfare (ASW) School. Much to the chagrin of her family (fearing she would "never finish college"), Annabel took a leave of absence in her last semester before graduation. We loaded our "worldly possessions" into our first car (a 1951 blue Dodge Wayfarer) and headed south – way south. We managed to find an affordable motel room ($50 per week) and have a wonderful two months in Key West and environs despite living on a tight budget (the Navy did not reimburse for TAD – temporary additional duty – expenses until *after* the duty concluded). Fortunately, movies on the Key West Naval Base cost only ten cents, a candy bar was four cents, and fish were plentiful and easy to catch. We met Lt. (jg) Lennie Levine and his wife Edith, neighbors at the motel, and shared Dinty Moore Beef Stew, played penny poker, and enjoyed the local beaches together. Lennie and I were in the same class at ASW School so we car-pooled and studied together.

After a post-ASW School holiday leave I returned to Norfolk, newly promoted to Lieutenant Junior Grade and now ASW Officer aboard *Owen*. Annabel returned to Brooklyn College to finish her last semester and the ship deployed to the Sixth Fleet in the Mediterranean.

This was strictly an ASW operation as we were part of the

Hal & Annabel, and Edith & Lennie Levine Boca Chica Beach, Key West – 1953

destroyer escort for the USS *Gilbert Islands* (CVE 107), an escort carrier built near the end of WWII. The Navy was just getting into the business of utilizing dipping sonar-equipped helicopters as part of the airborne ASW team, and this cruise was a precursor to the subsequent conversion of *Essex*-class CVAs to CVSs and the creation of "Hunter-Killer" Task Groups. Rear Adm. Fitzhugh Lee, a recipient of the Navy Cross for heroism in the Battle of Leyte Gulf as skipper of the USS *Manila Bay* (CVE61), was our Task Group Commander.

Liberty ports included Algiers, Genoa, Cannes, and Athens (Piraeus). In Cannes we were greeted by a large sign on the quay, "AMERICANS GO HOME!" The Communists in Western Europe were still very much a factor to be dealt with. We got over our annoyance as we were welcomed by wealthy Americans whose yachts were tied up in the harbor. Lt. Al Sprague (who subsequently commanded a minesweeper I visited years later in Guantánamo) and I found ourselves welcomed aboard Errol Flynn's yacht for drinks. The actor was not there, however we met the singer, Frances Langford, who was famous for her work on the Bob Hope Show and entertaining troops with him during WWII.

Annabel was now pregnant with Judy, but finished classes and graduated as the ship was returning to Norfolk for overhaul in the shipyard.

Among the exercises that were mandatory in those days before entering a drydock for hull repairs was an at-sea structural test. This consisted of the ship proceeding at slow speed while firing off a full pattern of depth charges, abeam and astern. All hatches were battened down for maximum water-tight integrity and all hands were at battle stations with helmets and life vests. The exploding depth bombs literally lifted the stern of the ship into the air and the entire ship shuddered and vibrated. Fortunately, no major leaks were noted. On reflection, the risky structural test was arguably one of the more stupid exercises dreamed up by shore-bound engineers.

Entering port – Sea Detail

The Norfolk Naval Shipyard is actually located in Portsmouth, Virginia, and is home to the historic "Dry-dock 1," which played a major role in the outfitting of Confederate ships during the Civil War, including the famous USS *Virginia* that became the *Merrimac.* We moved to a furnished apartment in Norfolk. This was really our first opportunity to "play house" and Annabel took pleasure in hosting elaborate dinners for junior officers who kindly relieved me of duty in order that I could spend more evenings at home.

Annabel with Spanish Mackerel Catch, Key West – 1953

Nights spent aboard ship in the shipyard were pure torture: no air conditioning, berthing spaces all torn up for such repairs as reinsulation of piping. Of course it wasn't until many years later that we realized we had been breathing in asbestos without an inkling of the dangers involved.

THE NEW SKIPPER, Cdr. Hubbell, soon became a favorite of the officers. A Georgia Tech graduate, Les commanded a destroyer in WWII at age 28. Now a senior Commander, he was not about to allow petty annoyances to keep him from thoroughly enjoying his second tour in command. What follows relates an event that caused more than petty annoyance and almost resulted in the loss of the ship.

Shortly before the completion of our overhaul, the ship, which had been emptied of fuel on arrival, was scheduled for an evening refueling. This was a routine procedure under the supervision of a petty officer trained in the transfer of fuel from tank to tank. His unofficial title is "oil king." The senior petty officer so designated decided to take the evening off, leaving the task to a junior petty officer. I was the Command Duty Officer, the senior officer with the watch on board for the 24-hour period 0800 to 0800. We were moored starboard side, too, alongside the pier. At the appropriate time, the word was passed: "The smoking lamp is out throughout the ship during fueling operations." Fueling commenced. Within 20 minutes, the ship began listing to starboard. After a short while, the list became pronounced and I rushed to the quarterdeck and had the word passed: "Cease fueling operations! Cease fueling operations!"

It turned out that a shipyard worker had neglected to reinstall an inspection plate over one of the main starboard wing tanks. Fuel was taken into the ready service tank and then transferred to the wing tank. With the inspection plate removed, the fuel spilled into the berthing space above it, causing the ship to list. The duty engineer and the duty oil king rushed up and suggested pumping the fuel to the port side. I fortunately remembered enough of my damage control training to know that once set in motion in the other direction with no fuel, water, stores or ammunition ballast, the ship would tend to keep rolling until it rolled over. I called the shipyard duty officer and requested a barge to come alongside and pump the fuel out of the starboard side. I then called the Captain. He rushed back to the shipyard and I explained what had happened and what action I had taken. Frankly frightened by what his reaction might be, I was immensely relieved to receive his "well done," for taking the right action and avoiding a possible disaster. Of course, the oil that flooded the crew's berthing space ruined their uniforms and they had to be compensated.

The senior oil king was reduced in rank for leaving the first fueling to an inexperienced hand.

Judy was born September 26, 1954, at the Portsmouth Naval Hospital. I was not there for the occasion; following overhaul, the ship had deployed for refresher training in Guantánamo Bay, Cuba. (It is often joked that a Naval Officer must be present for the laying of the keel, but not for the launching.) I was a very concerned prospective father, at sea in more ways than one, until I was handed a "class Easy" message that Judith Merry Sacks had arrived and that mother and daughter were doing well.

In October we learned that *Owen* was to be transferred permanently to the Pacific Fleet and those who preferred to remain on the East coast would be assigned to another ship. With a newborn, the Sacks family opted not to move to California and I was subsequently ordered to the USS *Stickell* (DDR 888), a radar picket destroyer home-ported in Norfolk. I reported aboard in early January 1955 and was assigned duties as ASW Officer and Fire Control Officer, responsible for the

USS *Stickell* (DDR 888)

men and equipment used to acquire and track air and surface gunnery targets.

Life aboard *Stickell* was fairly routine as no major deployments took place during the year I was aboard, although I did have an opportunity to sharpen my ship handling ability. Notable are two ports of call, New Orleans and Miami, during which Annabel's mom, Ruth, cared for Judy so Annabel could join me for a few days. Other port visits included Pensacola; Savannah (where

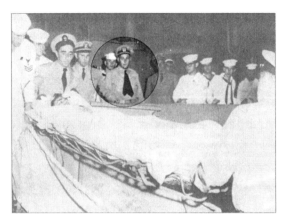

Injured pilot leaves the _Stickell_

I was privileged to have lunch with the great WWII heroes, Generals "Chesty" Puller and Mark Clark); and St. John, New Brunswick, Canada. Most importantly, Annabel and I decided to try to make a career of the Navy. I applied for augmentation from reserve to regular Navy at a time when the Navy was cutting back sharply. Fortunately, I was accepted.

Having fulfilled his initial three-year tour aboard destroyers, Lt. (jg) Sacks, USN, was ordered in January, 1956, to the heavy cruiser USS _Des Moines_ (CA 134).

THE THREE SHIPS of the _Salem_-class cruisers, (_Newport News_ was the third) were probably the most beautiful cruisers ever built. They were exceptional gun ships with rapid fire 8'55" turrets and half a dozen 5'38" twin mounts as well. These ships had a unique engineering set-up with each engineering space having a boiler and engine combined; in a sense we were always cross-connected.

The cruiser-battleship Navy was a world away from the relaxed and collegial tin can Navy of destroyers. Spit and polish prevailed and "rank had its privileges". In 1956 I had to purchase a ceremonial sword because officers in _Des Moines_ were required to wear them on formal occasions.

I was assigned duty as Operations Information Officer (OI Division), responsible for about 90 men who manned the Combat

Information Center (CIC), the Electronic Intercept equipment, and the Aerology Department. My immediate superior, Lt. Jim Brunson, put me in charge of radar navigation, an experience that proved to be an essential contribution to my future in the Navy. *Des Moines*, affectionately known as "Daisy Mae", headed for Northern Europe on a summer midshipman cruise. Third Class (plebes) and First Class Midshipmen in the Naval Academy were heading out for eight weeks of intensive training at sea. Our first port of call was Stockholm, Sweden, where junior officers were assigned to appear at one or more of the extravagant receptions planned by our Swedish hosts. It was at one of these

USS *Des Moines* (CA 134)

that the Captain's wife (who had met the ship in Stockholm) asked me to dance. While dancing she whispered the following in my ear, "You rascal, you! You did it again. Annabel is expecting a baby next winter."

Upon our return I was ordered to a five-week Air Intercept Controller's (AIC) school in Brunswick, Georgia. We trained with sub-sonic jets of the F2H variety, and I qualified easily, taking to the jargon and mastering the intercept techniques. Judy was a devilishly cute two-year-old, Annabel was now visibly pregnant, and the three and a half of us lived on Saint Simon's Island, right off the coast of Georgia. We fished for and picked a lot of crabs and enjoyed life on the beaches. On my return to the ship I was promoted to Lieutenant, and prepared for the birth of what we hoped would be a boy. February 8, 1957, our son, Stewart Jonathan Sacks (known as a child as "Skippy" and as an adult as Skip) was born, to our great excitement and joy. To celebrate, *Des Moines* left in March for a three-month Mediterranean war games cruise.

Assigned to permanent shore patrol in Genoa, Italy, I spent a lot of time on the Via San Benedetti, where one of the more popular spots was Ginny's 3 for 1 Hideaway ("buy 3 drinks, get 1 free"). Because it was only a few blocks from the fleet landing, it was among the first and last places our sailors and marines visited – and the shore patrol was called upon regularly to break up fights. On Christmas Eve 1957, the owner of the bar, Ginny DeLucia, an expatriate Italian-American, asked me to be at her bar by 11:00 PM. By the time we showed up, she had cut off pouring drinks and was passing out trays of sandwiches and coffee, sobering up the sailors and marines. We then assisted her in herding the whole lot across the street to a tiny Catholic church for midnight mass. The church was filled with shabby worshippers, so the gang filled up the vestibule. We were packed so closely together that even the unsober were held up by the others. But when they passed the plate, the sailors and marines displayed their generosity and the little church had its best collection of the year.

Ginny rewarded me by lending me her Maserati Sportster for two days while I was on liberty. She offered me one of her "girls" to go with the car but I went off with a shipmate, 1st Lt. Will Forey, USMC, instead.

British Canberra Bomber

IT'S DIFFICULT TO RECALL all the building blocks of a successful career in the Navy; however, some stand out in one's memory. On this particular Mediterranean cruise, we were assigned the role of defender against enemy strategic bombers. The Royal Air Force was flying Canberra jet bombers as the "Red" force. I was controlling F3H "Fury" interceptors, the first swept-wing jet fighter built by McDonnell Aircraft. Unfortunately, my

F3H Demon Fighter

interceptors' speed was only about 20 knots greater than the speed of the bombers. Thus, our intercept had to be "smack on" to result in a "talley ho!" The Canberras had a nasty habit of hiding in the land mass to confuse our radars and then popping out at the last minute, giving us little time to react. On more than one occasion, however, I was able to "dead reckon" their track across such places as the island of Corsica and have my interceptor in position to pounce. *Des Moines* had the best intercept record in the fleet during these war games.

ONE OF MY COLLATERAL DUTIES was as Electronic Countermeasures (ECM) Officer. We had just received the latest piece of ECM equipment (AN/SLR-2) and a new Fleet Tactical Publication (FXP) with instructions on how to coordinate ECM searches in a fleet situation. We experimented with the equipment in the Mediterranean and I developed a paper on the subject that became fleet doctrine.

As Aerology Officer I supervised a Petty Officer 3rd Class who manned the weather shack located two decks above the main deck aft. Each morning I was required to brief the Captain on the weather for the day based on information the petty officer derived from an antiquated machine that printed weather maps. I would report to the bridge and telephone the weather shack for the most current information. After several embarrassing incidents of faulty weather reports, I convinced my "weatherman" to just look out the porthole and let me know if it was raining, overcast, or sunny.

In the spring of 1957, I had served 18 months in the Cruiser navy, and we were ordered to duty overseas in Guantánamo Bay, Cuba (GTMO), I as a Shipboard Instructor/Inspector with the Fleet Training Group (FTG). When I arrived at my next duty station, I found myself instructing the fleet in Radar Navigation, Air Intercept Control, and Electronic Countermeasures and, of course, Gunfire Support, based on my Korean War experience.

Shopping in Genoa

★ ★ ★

The GTMO Years

Guantanamera, guajira guantanamera,
Guantanamera....

GUANTANAMO BAY (GTMO) was not a strange place to me. I was there for refresher training in 1954 aboard my first ship, USS *Owen* (DD536), when daughter Judy was born in the Navy hospital in Portsmouth. I was there again aboard the *Daisy Mae* during Operation Springboard in 1956. All I knew about GTMO were the grueling training days, the copious Bacardi Añejo rum punches at the Officers' Club, and the bargains at the Navy Exchange (Rolex watches were $95 in 1954). But the thought of a two-year tour of duty there with the Fleet Training Group (FTG) never occurred to me. It was, for all practical purposes, shore duty in that I would generally be home with my family every night. But it was sea duty in that I would be riding ships daily, sweating buckets along with the crew.

The Guantánamo enclave was ceded for 99 years following American intervention in support of Cuban independence during the Spanish-American War ("Remember the *Maine*") of 1898. It was initially a coaling station for the U.S. Fleet, and subsequently the finest training facility available to the East Coast Navy. A broad, natural, deepwater harbor capable of berthing or mooring any Navy ship from the smallest minesweeper to the largest super carrier, GTMO, located on the southeastern end of Cuba, was blessed with virtually 365 days per year of clear weather. Within 20 minutes of clearing harbor, our ships were in over 600 feet of water, able to conduct ASW operations, live anti-aircraft and surface gun firing exercises, and a myriad of engineering casualty drills.

The base itself was home to about 5,000 – military, their dependents, civilian employees and their dependents, along with an entrenched cadre of Cuban civil servant employees who did everything from bookkeeping to manual labor. There were about 70 miles of paved roads, a sandy golf course, two airfields, a petting zoo with two deer and two peacocks, and a full complement of clubs, pools, Navy exchange and commissary. All the departments – Public Works, Supply, Security, etc. – felt that life in Guantánamo would be idyllic were it not for the Fleet Training Group (FTG) and all the housing and services it required. Of course, without the FTG there would be no need for all the support departments.

Commanding the heights of the base was Crane Hill, named after the American author Stephen Crane, who served as a correspondent for the Hearst chain of newspapers during the Spanish-American War. From the top of Crane Hill, on a clear night, one could see the lights of Haiti, 80 miles away.

To anyone arriving in Havana, it was immediately obvious from the number of heavily-armed soldiers that the despotic regime of Dictator Fulgencio Batista was nervous about the increasing guerilla activities of Fidel Castro and his insurgents. I managed to get space aboard a Cubana Airlines DC3 which made several stops enroute the civilian airport serving Guantánamo City. At Victoria de las Tunas, the aircraft buzzed the field as a signal of its arrival, at which point a squad of white-capped nuns raced onto the field to shoo the cattle off the grass strip, enabling us to land. Later, approaching our final destination, the pilot banked the aircraft steeply, threading his way between the peaks of the Sierra Maestra Mountains.

Upon reporting for duty I learned that there would be a wait of about three months for housing before Annabel and the children could join me. I became part of a small group of real and "geographic" bachelors at Bachelor Officer Quarters (BOQ) Three, and went to work. "Ship riders" (the Instructor/Inspectors), reported aboard their ride for the day thirty minutes before the ship got underway, usually around 0600. They departed after the ship moored and received a critique of the exercises monitored, usually at around 1800. It was demanding work and the most professionally satisfying and useful work I had experienced thus far in the Navy. Of course, I rode destroyers, destroyer escorts, cruisers, minesweepers, and aircraft carriers. But exposure to tankers, attack cargo ships (AKA), ammunition ships (AE), coast guard cutters, aviation support vessels (AVP), merchant ships converted to early warning vessels (YAGR), landing ship docks (LSD), British, Dutch, and German ships, even sea-going tug boats, provided a broad understanding of ships that served as an important building block in my naval career.

Annabel arrived three months later with three-year-old

Judy, Skip and Annabel

Judy and seven-month-old Skippy and we settled into an old but spacious apartment in a quadriplex unit (with adjacent garage and servants' quarters) on Radio Point, just a quarter of a mile from FTG headquarters. Our family began almost two years of joyful employment, social life, and family togetherness. We had a rich life Jewishly, as well.

I had, while in USS *Des Moines*, organized a Passover Seder while the ship was enroute to the Mediterranean. It was attended by 25 to 30 Jewish crew members plus the Captain and the Admiral commanding the battleships and cruisers of the Atlantic Fleet (COMBATCRULANT). Its success was due in large measure to the supply of matzos, wine and traditional Passover foods supplied by the Jewish Welfare Board (JWB), predecessor of the JCCA, the current umbrella organization of Jewish Community Centers. The head of the Chaplaincy Division was Rabbi Aryeh Lev who became my connection and one-person support group for lay leader activities until his passing.

A SIGN AT THE FOOT of Chapel Hill (on which stood the non-denominational Christian chapel) indicated the times of Catholic Mass and Protestant Church services. I met with the head Chaplain and asked that a sign be added:

JEWISH SERVICES

8:00 PM

Every Friday Night

The sign was important since Jewish sailors from ships in training would pass it on their way to the various Enlisted Men's Clubs. Additionally, the weekly bulletin sent from the base commander to the ships included news of our services. The head chaplain even arranged for the covering of Christian symbols in the chapel on Friday night.

We soon attracted a group of sailors each week

which added to the ten or twelve Jewish families (a number of whom were doctors at the base hospital) who became regular attendees and good friends. We adjourned after services to an *Oneg Shabbat* (dessert and conversation) at one of our homes, and men who came one week were certain to be invited for *Shabbat* dinner the following week. Our commissary

Annabel's mom enters from Cuba on a visit

noted a small surge in the demand for beef brisket, and Annabel's mom kept us supplied with egg barley. At Rosh Hashanah, Rabbi Lev arranged for a rabbi to be activated from the Naval Reserve and sent to conduct services. At Passover we were on our own but received mountains of Passover food and wine from JWB and conducted great Seders at the Marine Family Restaurant on the base. It was always a kick to observe the Cuban waiters don *yarmulkes* and sing Passover songs during the clean-up after the families left.

Lasting friendships were made at GTMO, notably Jim and Barbara Chesky, and their sons Kim and Jay, dear friends of our family for over half a century. Cdr "Ham" Gentry was my boss. Ham was a very avuncular Texan who took a liking to us, supported me professionally, and greatly eased our acceptance into base society. Lt. Art Pearl, his wife Lorraine, and their two children, about the same age as ours, were good

The Jim Chesky family

friends. Art was a physician at the Naval Hospital, along with Mel Muceles, a pediatrician who subsequently made Admiral and took care of Linda Baines Johnson's baby. Art would fly on med-evacs to Miami where his family loaded him down with kosher deli and appetizing[1] and we were always invited over to share.

ANDY AND JUDY SPIELMAN were shipmates during what were to be the last joyful years in GTMO – before Fidel Castro's revolu-tion, based in the adjacent Sierra Maestra Mountains, overthrew Fulgencio Batista and seized power on January 1, 1959. Andy, a Medical Service Corps officer, was the base entomologist. As lieutenants with growing families, we lived in what can best be termed "genteel poverty," replete with live-in maid service, $1 prime rib dinners at the Marine Family Restaurant, 10-cent happy hours at the Officer's Club, and occasional weekend visits as "space available" guests aboard Navy ships to Ocho Rios, Kingston or Montego Bay, Jamaica; Port au Prince, Haiti; and the Panama Canal Zone.

Andy and I became good friends, and he invited me to join him on several of his entomological field trips. Some of his research involved gnats, those tiny but annoying varieties that

[1]Appetizing: The name given to foods bought at what used to be called "appetizing stores." These stores were basically non-meat delicatessens, featuring a variety of smoked fish, pickled herring, cheese and other dairy products, and wonderful homemade sauerkraut and kosher dill pickles.

swarm around ankles and eyes. His gnat traps provided the evidence needed to prove that the eye-gnats and the ankle-gnats were actually different species. Andy discovered a new species of lizard, eponymously surnamed *spielmaniensis*. His mosquito traps demonstrated that the mosquito that bit you as the sun was setting was a different species than the one that bit you when

Lt. Andy Spielman and family

the lights were out in the bedroom at night. Ultimately, it was the special assignment to protect our Douglas A4D Skyhawks from the threat of buzzards that made a lasting impression on both of us.

I HAVE REGALED friends with the details of the following adventure for almost half a century. McCalla Field, the traditional airstrip at GTMO, was where the propeller-driven aircraft took off and landed. The planes were predominantly the durable twin-engine WWII B-26 reconfigured as JDs for AA gunnery target sleeve towing, to be deployed for Combat Air Patrol (CAP) and a myriad of other training chores. The entrance to the terminal sported a sign, "Through These Portals Pass the Best Cross Wind Aviators in the World." Yes, the prevailing winds tended to cross the runway at right angles.

Across the bay, however, was Leeward Point, the jet air strip, and GTMO residents close to shore were deafened by the roar of jet engines during flight ops. On the same side of the bay was Hicacl Beach, a strip paralleling the west end of

Art Pearl and Hal sailing in Grenadilla Bay

Guantánamo Bay that delineated the low-level bombing run of Navy and Marine A4D light attack bombers. They were a joy to watch, screaming in at low altitude ("on the deck"), then shooting almost straight up, tossing the bomb (which could frequently be seen reflected by sunlight) and then rolling over, diving to the deck and departing.

Andy received a call from the aviation commander at Leeward Point. Buzzards were riding the convection currents in the flight path of the A4s and there was real concern that one would be sucked into the air intake causing damage and possibly the loss of an aircraft, not to mention the pilot (the danger of ingesting birds threatened jet aircraft long before the "Miracle on the Hudson" almost 50 years later in 2009). When Andy invited me to join him the next day on a field trip, I eagerly accepted. As his jeep labored on the rough road alongside the boundary fence, Andy explained that buzzards needed two things to exist: a place to roost and a supply of food. Our mission was to identify both.

By mid-morning we had reached the ruins of the old coaling station, just past the mangrove swamps on Toro Cay – if memory serves me correctly, a relic of the Spanish-American War. Climbing about twenty feet up a rusted steel ladder to the top of the concrete ruins, we could see two walled concrete enclosures, each about forty feet square. One was open at the top revealing concrete pillars about 12 to 18 inches square. The pillars were the answer to one question: They were the perfect roosting facilities for buzzards. The other was totally closed at the top except for a steel hatch cover about two feet in diameter.

Andy ran ahead over the top of the enclosed structure and began wrestling with the hatch cover which refused to move. Finally, together we were able to slide the cover past the opening – about the size of a manhole. We were greeted by a frightening – to me – rush of thousands of bats which screeched past us. When their exodus ended Andy immediately started down the inside ladder into the black hole. Too embarrassed to verbalize my horror at descending into a pitch-dark hole from which bats had recently emerged, I followed him without a word. We shone our flashlights on the walls which were still almost covered with clinging bats, and were almost knocked over by the stench. Andy estimated there were two to three feet of bat guano at the bottom. I took his word for it. Thus, the second question was answered. Bats provided our buzzards

Guantánamo Bay viewed from Stephen Crane Hill

NAVAL COMMAND NETHERLANDS ANTILLES
HEADQUARTERS OF THE COMMANDER IN CHIEF
WILLEMSTAD, CURACAO

Security classification: Date: August, 16th 1958
                                                  Nr: 8616/662/CZMNA

From:

To: Rear Admiral R. B. Ellis
       Commander Naval Base Guantanamo Bay,
       US fleet mail office, Guantanamo bay,
       Cuba

Subject:

Enclosures:

Sir,

I have the greatest pleasure in writing you to express my most grateful
thanks for the services rendered to H.Neth.M.S. "Van Speijk" during the
working-up period from july 10th - 28th 1958.

The exercises have been most valuable to the officers and men and improved the ship's effectiveness to a great deal.

I also learned that the assistance, provided by the officers and men of
Fleet training group, contributed highly to the proper execution of the
exercises and you would oblige me, by conveying my sincere thanks in
this respect to the Commander fleet training group.

The warm hospitality, shown to the officers and men has also been much
appreciated. Please accept my greatest appreciation for the facilities
and arrangements made during the visit of H.Neth. M.S. "Van Speijk".

                     I have the honour to be, Sir,

                          Yours faithfully
                 commander in chief Netherlands Antilles,

                          /s/H.A.W. Goossens,
                            H.A.W. Goossens,
                              commodore

080/082:

**Commendatory letter placed in my jacket by the
Fleet Training Group commander**

FLEET TRAINING GROUP, GUANTANAMO BAY
TRAINING COMMAND, U. S. ATLANTIC FLEET
NAVY 115, BOX 55
C/O FLEET POST OFFICE
NEW YORK, N. Y.

In reply refer to:
FF8-6/GTMO/05:ko
566469/1100
17 September 1958

From: Commander Fleet Training Group, Guantanamo Bay, Cuba
To: Lieutenant Harold H. SACKS, USN

Subj: Services rendered to H. Neth. M. S. "Van Speijk" during
working-up period from July 10th through 28th 1958

Ref: (a) CINC Netherlands Antilles ltr 8616/662/CZMNA of 16 Aug 1958,
with first end thereto

1. Reference (a) (copy attached) expressed the thanks of the Commander
in Chief of the Naval Command, Netherlands Antilles, for the services
rendered in working-up H. Neth. M. S. "Van Speijk" during the period
July 10th through 28th, 1958.

2. During this period you were assigned as an instructor in the CIC
department and your effective supervision, instruction and spirit of
helpfulness were instrumental in assisting "Van Speijk" in her training.

3. It gives me great pleasure to commend you for your performance of
duty, not only in assisting the ship but in cementing cordial relations
between the United States Navy and a unit of the navy of one of our
NATO allies.

G. R. WILSON

with an ample food supply. Yummy!

In due course, the bats were eliminated (doubtless in a manner not likely to be approved today by People for the Ethical Treatment of Animals [PETA] or wildlife conservationists); the roosts were knocked down; the buzzards departed (for lack of food, no doubt); the A4s continued their bombing practice in safety.

Andy and I lost touch after leaving GTMO. I moved on to my next tour and Andy was off to Harvard to begin his illustrious career in insect-borne diseases. He became arguably *the* preeminent worldwide expert on mosquito-borne diseases. It was his service in the Navy which ultimately led to his pioneering work in understanding the transmission of Lyme disease, his investigation of the role of the mosquito in transmitting malaria and dengue fever, and his directorship of the malaria epidemiology program at the Harvard Center for International Development.

Andy and I reconnected after all the intervening years in November, 2006. He promised to send me a copy of his benchmark book, *Mosquitoes*. I was not aware that he was suffering from a form of chronic leukemia. Apparently, he still maintained his frenetic pace, traveling worldwide – as he had for five decades – from Mauritius to Cuba, from Israel to Jordan and beyond. I was greatly saddened to read, in the obituary section of the *New York Times* on December 22, 2006, of the passing of Dr. Andrew Spielman. After his funeral, his colleague found a copy of *Mosquitoes* on his desk, inscribed to me. He sent it to me – and I have it still.

Senior Chief Fire Control Technician Wall, Lieutenant Joe Dalpian and I were a team of three instructor/inspectors working together during gunfire exercises. Joe worked with the gun mounts and directors, Chief Wall in the plotting room with the fire control computer operators, and I in the Combat

Information Center (CIC) and on the bridge. Annabel was teaching kindergarten at the William T. Sampson School on the base, and one of her students was Alvin Wall, the Chief's son. Chief Wall passed away at an early age; however, his son Alvin is a Jewish community leader and the respected head of a large accounting firm in Norfolk which has handled our taxes for decades.

ONE INCIDENT relative to Castro's insurgency stands out in memory. Called upon every two or three months to serve as Shore Patrol Officer, I would ride a bus filled with pleasurebound sailors and marines from the Naval Base into Guantánamo City, a forty-minute trip. The bus was scheduled to return at midnight. On one particular night, about fifteen minutes before reaching the base, our still-celebrating sailors were quickly sobered by gunfire and the sound of windows shattering in the bus. One sailor was slightly wounded but we made it safely onto the base without further trouble. I immediately filled out my report and strongly recommended that no further buses be permitted to leave the base. This warning was ignored. The next night, the bus returning from Guantánamo City was kidnapped – and all its occupants taken to Castro's hideout in the nearby mountains. It fortunately turned out to be nothing more than an exciting adventure for the sailors; all were returned to the base safely after a few days. Of course, the result of the much-publicized incident was the closing of the "gate"; personnel who lived on the base were no longer permitted to drive into Cuba. We still wonder today about how life is in Guantánamo City, a small city with areas of architecture reminiscent of the French quarter of New Orleans.

Thus, we rounded out our days in "paradise." The family thrived. Judy learned to swim, dive and ride a "two-wheeler." Skippy was all boy, speaking as much Spanish as English.

However, among his first words in English were "Ro, ro," as he pointed to the ubiquitous cockroaches that resided, no matter the efforts to annihilate them, in all the old GTMO residences; among his first sentences in Spanish was "*Rosa* (our Cuban maid), *un vaso con leche, por favor*." ("Rosa, may I please have a glass of milk.").

When Cdr. Ham Gentry handed me my new orders to report to Destroyer Squadron (DESRON) 12 as Operations, ASW, and Gunnery Officer, he commented, "You are in for it now, my boy. Your Commodore will be Captain John D. Bulkeley, the WWII hero who rescued General Macarthur and his family from the Philippines, sank two Japanese cruisers, and is one of the toughest sons of bitches in the United States Navy." (A number of years later, as COMNAVBASE GTMO, Admiral Bulkeley, with much ceremony, cut the water pipe from the Yateras River to GTMO, having fired up the desalinization plant on the base.)

In June, 1959, we packed up, left GTMO (although I was to return many times), enjoyed a month's leave with our families, and settled in to a very small rented home in Portsmouth, Rhode Island, adjacent to Newport, home port of Destroyer Squadron (DESRON) 12.

CHAPTER FIVE

★　★　★

The Newport Navy

WE LEFT OUR OLD DODGE Coronet in Cuba. (When I returned on a humanitarian mission fifty years later, I half expected to find it still chugging around the streets of Havana along with other vintage autos.) Returning to the "real world" in the USA, we faced an economic quandary. We needed a new car, winter clothes, a washer and replacements for all the appliances abandoned in GTMO. Thus, we settled on renting a small house in Portsmouth, Rhode Island, a rural town three miles from Newport.

When I call it a small house, I do mean small. It had three bedrooms and we could plug the vacuum cleaner into an outlet in the living room and vacuum the

Our house in Rhode Island after a winter storm

entire house without moving the plug. The rent was reasonable. However, the house was owned by a woman whose father had been a nurseryman, and our lease required that we maintain the shrubs. "Landscape management" became a full-time job during the rare periods I was not at sea.

As warned by Cdr. Ham Gentry, my early encounters with Captain John D. Bulkeley, the squadron Commodore, were tense. I had just published an article in the U.S. Naval Institute *Proceedings* on "Anti-intellectualism in the Navy" (September 1959) and I knew that Bulkeley, an engineer at heart, viewed me as a "smart-ass New York Jew" from the outset. Fortunately, he was fairly out of touch with operational matters and was forced to rely on me. We established a pattern whereby he chewed me out vigorously in public and would invite me to his cabin to share an apple and cheese in the evening, his way of apologizing. Slowly, out of mutual professional respect, an affectionate father-son relationship developed, one which lasted well past his tour as COMDESRON 12.

Illustrative of this relationship was the incident of the collision of the USS *Bristol*, DD 857, the last of seventy *Sumner*-class destroyers built during WWII, with the merchant ship *Itala Fazio* in a pea-soup fog off Block Island. *Bristol* was one of the ships in our squadron and the skipper, Cdr. Bergen, was one of the few our "Squad Dog" liked. The basic facts of the incident were that a very junior Officer of the Deck (OOD) on *Bristol* failed to keep the Captain notified of the tactical picture and by the time the Captain was summoned on deck, it was too late to avoid a collision; all he could do was reverse engines and thus minimize the impact. Since this happened on a weekend, all the admirals in Newport had bailed out and Captain Bulkeley, who was living aboard ship, was left to deal with the situation. Bulkeley was appointed a one-man Board of Investigation and it was his job to sort things out. *Bristol* had limped into the Boston Navy Yard for repairs (happily, there were no injuries on either ship) and I was dispatched immediately to Boston to reconstruct the events leading up to the collision.

I gathered up the quartermaster's rough deck log which

included: the lookout's report; the Combat Information Center (CIC) Bearing Book listing the radar bearings taken on the Italian vessel; the CIC track chart Dead Reckoning Tracer (DRT) display; the Engine Order Telegraph Log, a record of all engine speed commands maintained by the forward engine room; and went to work. The tracks of both ships were reconstructed and it was clear that the ships had been on a steady bearing at decreasing range for about forty minutes. The OOD mistakenly thought the bearings were drifting to starboard (right) and made the disastrous move of changing course to port (left) at the last minute. The *Itala Fazio* turned to starboard at the same time and both ships, now visible to each other, reversed engines and sounded their alarms. It was a classic case. The Navy ship was obligated under the Rules of the Nautical Road to have turned to starboard and was clearly in the wrong. The Italian ship, however, never reduced speed and was tracked (by me) proceeding at high speed in a dense fog and was thus partially in the wrong.

Unlike most automobile accidents wherein one party is deemed to be in the wrong, maritime law generally considers both parties to be equally at fault if one is as little as ten percent responsible. Thus, I had provided a basis for equal fault.

The formal hearing was in a Navy courtroom in Boston. I drove up with Annabel and the children as we were to leave right after the hearing for the Rosh Hashanah holiday in New York. Captain Bulkeley was on the bench with his Navy Judge Advocate General (JAG) lawyer. Cdr. Bergen was flanked by his own Navy JAG lawyers, as was the OOD. I was called to the stand as an "expert witness." Most of the morning was spent with tedious rounds of negotiation as to how my charts and logs should be entered into evidence. It soon approached noon and one of the JAG lawyers suggested a recess before I was called to the stand. My heart sank as I thought of my family waiting, and hopes of arriving in New York in time for the holiday meal grew dim. Then

Bulkeley amazed me. He declared that Lt. Sacks had to depart in order to be home for the Jewish holiday and there would be no recess until after he had testified.

Judy and Skippy loving the snow after two years in GTMO

Once I was on the stand, Cdr. Bergen's attorney questioned my credentials as an expert witness. Again, Bulkeley amazed me. Before I could answer, he said that Lt. Sacks had just returned from two years as an instructor/inspector in radar navigation and was considered to be one of the three or four leading experts in radar navigation in the entire United States Navy (a stretch at best). Nonetheless, I was able to establish the mutual fault of both vessels which ultimately formed the basis of the Navy saving several millions of dollars in its final negotiations with the *Itala Fazio*'s insurance company. The young OOD received a reprimand for failing to keep the skipper informed as his night orders directed, and Cdr. Bergen's career was not damaged. Annabel had the car waiting outside the court and we made it to New York in time for the traditional brisket dinner.

A VISIT TO THE COMMODORE'S cabin in USS *Blandy* (DD 937), the flagship of DESRON Twelve, was a trip in itself. Captain Bulkeley would frequently be in his pajamas and robe, a robe on which were embroidered a few of his award ribbons, such as the Medal of Honor, the Navy Cross, and the Army's Distinguished Service Cross. He generally had parts of an engine or pump leaking oil on the already stained carpet and considerable space was taken up by a printing press on which he did his own stationery and calling cards. The knife he cut the aforementioned apple with was a four-inch-bladed hunting knife worn in a sheath at his belt. As he walked about the ship he would use that knife to cut off any "Irish pennants" (frayed threads from canvas gun covers and the like). After collecting a small handful he would visit the stateroom of the ship's executive officer and unceremoniously dump them on his desk.

The destroyer base in Newport had recently experienced the implementation of a smartness program. Bound in green and known as "the Green Hornet," or in some cases as "the Green Weenie," the instruction sought to end the sloppiness that had crept in following WWII and the Korean War. Thus at 0800 each morning, with the raising of Colors, the Command Duty Officer was directed personally to stand at the ensign and the Junior Officer of the Day was to be a precise number of feet behind the Union Jack on the forecastle. Bulkeley would head to the bridge just before colors with his binoculars and scan each ship in his squadron for any infraction. The delinquent duty officer would receive a memo to report to the commodore's cabin at once. Trembling and perspiring profusely, the terrified young officer would appear. Bulkeley, all charm, would introduce himself, shake the young man's hand warmly, mildly reproach him and hand him two drink tickets good at the officer's club. A greatly relieved Bulkely fan for life would then depart.

In those days, each ship had a finite amount of operating expense money to fund consumable items. Highly pilferable items such as binoculars and foul weather jackets came under the title of "equipage" and their replacement required a survey report to explain their disappearance or their being worn beyond repair. Ships were always in the hole with equipage and so "Bulkeley's Raiders" went to work. The "Raiders" consisted of the commodore, the squadron engineer (Lcdr Lou Cowsert) and

Lt. Sacks. We requisitioned a pickup truck and, in tandem with the commodore's sedan, headed to the Boston Naval Shipyard where preparations were underway to scrap a WWII vintage CVE (Escort Aircraft Carrier). Sealed up and separately stored were its equipage items, and we signed for and brought back to Newport sufficient binoculars, chronometers, barometers, china, etc., to supply the entire squadron with replacements for missing items. Each ship received several cartons with a specially printed card attached (printed on Bulkeley's press) that read: COMPLIMENTS OF BULKELEY'S RAIDERS.

Bulkeley had a classic sports car, a Triumph TR3, which he parked in the long driveway of our little house when the squadron went to sea. When we returned he would usually come to dinner and play with the kids. Skippy, two years old, called him "Cap'n Buppy." The feared hero of WWII who sank two Japanese cruisers; rescued General Douglas MacArthur and his wife and son from the Philippines and carried them safely in a PT boat to Australia; guided a U.S. submarine carrying the Philippine government's gold supply through mined channels; recruited John F. Kennedy into the PT force; grounded his destroyer off Normandy in order to get within firing range of German targets; and was awarded the Congressional Medal of Honor, turned out to be a warm, if slightly eccentric, human being.

[Commodore Bulkeley humorously inscribed a number of photos to Annabel as though she had known him for decades, and wrote a series of letters, which I cherish, to members of the Sacks family. I include them on following pages.]

At Bulkeley's change of command, when he was relieved by Captain Alan Nibbs, the participants were surprised by the arrival of two unexpected guests, Chief of Naval Operations, Admiral Arleigh "31 Knot" Burke and retired reserve Rear Admiral John Ford, the famous movie director. Ford directed "They Were

COMMANDER DESTROYER SQUADRON TWELVE

28 June 1960

LT Harold H. SACKS, USN
Staff, Commander Destroyer Squadron TWELVE
Fleet Post Office
New York, New York

Dear Lieutenant SACKS:

I am deeply appreciative of your loyalty, marked abilities
and skills as an operations officer of DesRon 12. Without
them, we could have not made the achievements in the past
year that we have.

Your personal loyalty and devotion and friendship
has been a source of pride to me.

It has been a privilege to have had the pleasure
to serve with you. Thank you.

Most sincerely,

JOHN D. BULKELEY

The inscription is "to Annabel
with love, John D. Bulkeley,
Midshipman, First Class
May 31, 1933"
(at which time Annabel would
have been 5 months old)

"To Annabel with Love,
April 26, 1955,
John D. Bulkeley Captain"

"To Annabel with Love,
John D. Bulkeley, Lcdr, USN,
4 June, 1944"
with King George of England

"To Annabel with my
Admiration, John D. Bulkeley,
Captain, 20 August 1944"

COMMANDER DESTROYER SQUADRON TWELVE

28 June 1960

Mrs. Harold H. SACKS
44 Stagecoach Road
RFD #2
Newport, Rhode Island

Dear Mrs. SACKS:

I want you to know my appreciation for your most
kind, thoughtful and gracious hospitality to me during
the past year. It has been a real privilege to know
you and your very wonderful family. I only regret
that you did not drive the Blue Dragon Killer while she
was in your custody.

It has been a real pleasure and privilege to know
you and Hal.

Most sincerely,

JOHN D. BULKELEY

COMMANDING OFFICER
CLARKSVILLE BASE
CLARKSVILLE, TENNESSEE

19 June 1961

Lieutenant Commander Harold B. Sacks, USN
Staff, Destroyer Squadron TWELVE
% Fleet Post Office
New York, N. Y.

Dear Hal,

    Attached herewith is a copy of the letter that I wrote your father.
I am delighted to do it for both of you. You have a very wonderful
father and one to be very proud of.

    Also: Next printing session you will be listed as Scrounger in
Chief, Atlantic Fleet....also as "Chief See About Man" - the See About
Man is the gentleman that all hands see about something or other.

    Scrounging is good hereabouts. We have one very beautiful and
complete 28 foot steel craft yacht and also one 16 foot fiberglass
sloop for use on Kentucky Lake. Kentucky Lake is 184 miles long and
has a 12 mile beam..

Kindest regards,

BULKLEY

19 June 1961

Mr. Joseph Sacks
1925 Washington Avenue
Miami Beach, Florida

My dear Mr. Sacks,

I recently saw in the orders for Officers of the Navy that your
son Harold was being ordered to Intelligence School in Washington.
I think that you can now bask in the Miami sun as well as in pride
that this is a very choice assignment and augurs well for the
future of Hal.

I am sure that you are just as aware as I am of the significance
of intelligence in this world today. Your son has those attributes
for intelligence that may well be significant to the security of
the United States in the near future.

My congratulations, Sir.

                                        Very respectfully,

                                        BULKELEY

Expendable," the movie depicting Bulkeley's exploits, starring John Wayne and Robert Montgomery (who played Bulkeley).

Commodore Bulkeley at his Change of Command, May, 1960, with Rear Adm. John Ford, USNR

Ford arrived at the change of command in a midnight blue uniform, which stood out against all the dark blue uniforms of the officers. At the conclusion of the ceremony Bulkeley thanked all who served with him and, placing his arm around me added, "especially my right arm."

Years later, when (then) Rear Admiral Bulkeley became Commander of the Naval Base at Guantánamo Bay, Cuba, I was XO of the destroyer *Gyatt* undergoing refresher training at GTMO. I was invited to lunch with the Admiral and his family and greatly enjoyed the reunion. Bulkeley became famous for cutting off the water pipe from Cuba into the Base when Fidel Castro accused him of stealing water.

Squadron Twelve departed Newport in the summer of 1960 for a seven-month Mediterranean deployment. In those days, the Navy deployed three carrier task groups to the area along with three destroyer squadrons. Anti-air Warfare (AAW) and Anti-submarine Warfare (ASW) exercises were conducted with port visits to Genoa, Naples, Cannes, and Athens, among others. Electronic Countermeasure Exercises (ECM) were notable in that the procedures I helped develop while in the Mediterranean with USS *Des Moines* and utilized to train most East Coast Navy ships were now standard practice in the Fleet.

Without any doubt, the incursion of USS *Davis* (our flagship) and USS *H. R. Dickson* into the Black Sea was the highlight of the cruise. As Squadron Operations Officer I was charged with planning and preparing the operation order and arranging for the collection and reporting of any intelligence gained. The ships filed hundreds of Intelligence Reports (IRs) containing radar, ECM, visual, hydrographic and sonar information. The Director of Naval Intelligence commended Task Group 64.5 for its outstanding work. A detailed report in the form of an unpublished article written by me in 2009 is contained in Chapter Six, "Cold War Operations in the Black Sea."

Not long after our return from the seven month Mediterranean deployment, the ships of the squadron entered Boston Naval Shipyard for their biennial overhaul. An operations officer wasn't of much use to ships in drydock. So I was ordered to temporary duty in Newport as part of a curriculum writing team for the U.S. Navy Destroyer School, then under development. Headed by Captain Julian Lebourgeois (who went on to become a Vice Admiral, and President of the Naval War College) was a small team of lieutenants, each with expertise in one or more fields, naval engineering, gunnery, operations, ASW and so forth. A new six-month school was being created for "cut above"

**Lt. Harold H. Sacks
Memorial Day 1960**

destroyer division officers nominated by their skippers to prepare them for return to destroyers as department heads. I headed a small working group that prepared the curriculum for operations, consisting of Combat Information, and Com-munications (including radio, crypto, and visual signaling). With Captain Lebourgeois' encouragement, I wrote and had published in the U.S. Naval Institute Proceedings a major article introducing the Destroyer School to the Fleet.

Our two-year tour ended and so did nine years of continuous sea duty; time for the sailor to go ashore. Ordered to Washington DC for nine months of postgraduate studies at the Naval Intelligence School, we said farewell to friends and neighbors, packed up and moved to a larger house in District Heights, Maryland. Judy would enter the first grade; Skip would tear around in Air Force fatigues, and Annabel's brother, Marty, a post-doctoral scientist at the Naval Research Laboratory (NRL) would join our household for the next four years.

CHAPTER SIX

★ ★ ★

Cold War Operations in the Black Sea

0823, Sunday 2 October 1960, underway from Salamis, Greece, for Eregli, Turkey, in accordance with CTF 60 OP-ORDER 59-60. Winds light and variable, temperature 72 degrees, visibility unlimited.

THUS, USS *DAVIS* (DD 937) commanded by Cdr. Kent Rosemont with Captain Alan Nibbs, COMDESRON 12, and Staff embarked, proceeded to rendezvous with USS *Intrepid* (CVA 11) and USS *Harlan R. Dickson* (DD 708). The destroyers, after topping off fuel from *Intrepid* in the pre-dawn hours of October 3, were detached to proceed as Task Group 64.5 via the Dardanelles and the Straits of Bosporus to Eregli, home port of the Turkish Black Sea Fleet. Captain Nibbs was Commander Task Group 64.5 and I, as his Operations Officer, along with Lt. Frank Rentz, *Davis'* Operations Officer, had written the Operation Order under which we sailed.

The mission of TG 64-5 was three-fold: first, to exercise the right of free passage under the terms of the internationally recognized Montreux Convention of 1936 (to which, incidentally, the United States was not a signatory); second, to conduct intelligence collection operations utilizing ships' sensors – electronic, sonic, photographic and hydrographic. No communications intelligence collection was planned or authorized; third, to make courtesy visits to Turkish ports under the authority granted in Article 17 of the Montreux Convention.

This was to be only the second occasion in the fifteen years since the end of WW II that U.S. Navy warships would exercise such rights, but the context in which the operation was planned was fraught with tension. The Soviets had recently shot down two U.S. reconnaissance aircraft. At the United Nations, Soviet Premier Khrushchev, who in 1956 threatened to bury us, was only one week later pounding his shoe on the table at the U.N.'s New York building. The task group commander, his skippers and their crews did not know what awaited them when they entered the Black Sea. Greatly warmed by the wildly cheering Turkish gun crews waving huge American flags from their emplacements, the task group cranked on some knots and charged smartly into the "Russian Lake," making turns for 20 knots.

1106 – Temperature 69, light winds from the east at 7 knots, visibility 7 miles in slight haze, c/c to 090T, c/s to 12 knots.

WAS IT A MERE COINCIDENCE that *Davis*, the seventh ship of the Navy's last class of pure gunships, was met by what could be termed "sister ships" of the Soviet Black Sea Fleet? Five miles dead ahead was a *Kotlin*-class destroyer – like *Davis*, built in the 1950s, virtually identical in size, also the last pure gunnery destroyer built by the Soviets. And 30 degrees to starboard was another!

Davis and *Dickson* were to spend the afternoon and evening steaming independently with orders to approach the Crimean peninsula and the Romanian/Bulgarian coasts respectively,

USS *Davis* (DD 937)

collecting data enroute before heading southeast for Eregli, to rendezvous at 0630 for entering port on 4 October. The turn to the North energized our Kotlin escorts who closed to within 200 yards abeam. Just as our gunnery stations were manned in Readiness Condition III, it was apparent that the Soviets were similarly alert. It was also obvious that they were constrained, as we were, neither to train mounts or directors nor to lock on with fire control radar. ECM reported no fire control radar or air search radar emissions. Both U.S. and Soviet crews got a good look at each other and, aside from the intelligence photography concentrating on each ship's antennae, there were numerous examples of sailors taking photos of sailors taking photos.

Just after the changing of the watch at 1600, with the Kotlins back on station five miles abeam, sonar reported a contact evaluated as possible submarine. The 1AS exercise team was stationed and the contact was pursued until 1730, then lost. (Subsequent sonar contacts throughout the week were all classified non-sub.)

Davis and *Dickson* rendezvoused and formed up precisely on time, arriving at the port at 0801 and, after mooring, devoted the day and evening to calls made and returned by Commander Black Sea Base and COMDESRON TWELVE. Turkish Naval officers and enlisted petty officers entertained our officers and crew with an extravagant middle Eastern dinner and music. The Turkish English-language press headlined our visit, welcoming "U.S. Ambassadors of Freedom."

Upon getting underway at 0800 on October 5, our Kotlins were waiting and *Davis* headed for the port of Samsun while *Dickson* proceeded independently further east to Trabzon, site of a U.S. Air Force tracking station. The Soviets remained in visual distance throughout the day, splitting off, one with *Davis*, one with *Dickson*. Ships' companies continued the collection of hydrographic and electronic intelligence throughout the day and night before mooring precisely on schedule at 0800 on October 6.

In Samsun, hundreds of Turkish visitors toured the ship, limited in numbers only by the availability of boat transportation to our anchorage. We were feted by the Turkish army and initiated into their army's method of imbibing *raki*, a serious alcoholic beverage. Whether encouraged by the *raki* or not, we decided to play a little one-upmanship with the Soviet destroyers. CTG 64.5 asked CO *Davis* if he would be willing to light off all four boilers upon getting underway on October 7. CO *Davis* agreed as did CO *Dickson*.

The Soviet Kotlins, having patrolled through the night just offshore of Samsun and Trabzon respectively, were caught with their superheaters down and were left belching black smoke as *Davis* and *Dickson*, underway independently, making thirty-two plus knots, disappeared over the horizon. TG 64.5 conducted independent intelligence collection sweeps on October 7 and 8 prior to rendezvousing for departure from the Black Sea on the morning of October 9.

Looking back, the operation lacked the drama of later U.S. Navy experiences in the Black Sea (one is reminded of the ramming of USS *Yorktown* (CG48) by a Soviet *Krivak 1*-class frigate in February 1988.) However, to the young officers and crews of *Davis* and *Dickson*, this uncommon entry into the Black Sea was high adventure and a welcome departure from the Sixth Fleet routine involving three carrier task groups and twenty-four destroyers plus an assortment of heavy gun and missile cruisers.

Meanwhile, the Montreux Convention of 1936, which initially served to protect the Soviet Union from superior hostile fleets, appears to have created difficulties for the Soviets as they vastly expanded their fleets beginning in the mid-1960s. The Convention, for example, included special provisions for aircraft carriers, leading the Soviets to designate the Black Sea home-ported *Moskva*-class carriers as "aviation cruisers." The *Kiev*-class carrier, introduced in 1975, which carried a squadron of STOL aircraft and an expanded squadron of helicopters, was designated a "Large Antisubmarine Cruiser." Turkey, having repeatedly rejected Soviet demands to modify the Convention, nevertheless allowed these ships to transit into the Mediterranean in violation of its terms.

The Cold War may be over, but the enduring Montreux Convention continues to exert its influence over naval affairs. The United States attempted to dispatch the hospital ships USNS *Comfort* and USNS *Mercy* to Georgia following the end of the war with Russia over South Ossetia in September 2008. This was frustrated due to the Convention restriction of 45,000 aggregate tons. The relief ships, converted auxiliaries, weigh 69,000 tons and were not permitted through the Turkish Straits. The Navy *was* able to send USS *McFaul* (DDG 74), USCGC *Dallas* (WHEC 716), and the command ship USS *Mount Whitney* (LCC 20) into the Black Sea loaded with humanitarian supplies.

CHAPTER SEVEN

★ ★ ★

Stateside Shore Duty
PART 1

ANNABEL'S BROTHER, MARTY, a post-doctoral metallurgical engineer at the Naval Research Laboratory in Anacostia, found a three-bedroom rental house for us in District Heights, Maryland, just off the Pennsylvania Avenue Extension. We bade farewell to our neighbors in Rhode Island, shipped all our belongings south, and drove to Washington, hoping to arrive in time to meet the moving van. Unfortunately, the van broke down on the Delaware Memorial Bridge and all the furniture had to be off-loaded and reloaded (in the rain) onto another van. Annabel cried; the children were a little berserk; but we finally settled in (with Marty in the third bedroom) and I began studies at the Naval Intelligence School (NIS).

The first few months at NIS were very rigorous. An intensive introduction by the erudite Professor DeCelles, an expert in Soviet and Chinese geography, had us memorizing rivers, mountains, manufacturing zones and analyzing military capabilities. Since some of us upon graduation would be assigned as Naval Attachés, we learned how to take and process photographs without benefit of commercial developing services. Not that we would be "spies." However, utilizing the limited access we might be granted in an Iron Curtain country, we learned what to look for, how to report it, and how not to be thrown out of a country as *personae non grata.*

1961 saw the dawn of the digital computer age. The IBM 7090, the power supply for which took up a room half the size of a football field and was only about a fraction as powerful as a current laptop, had just been installed in Washington, requiring us to take a mini-course in computer programming. Field trips were made to military installations which were to be treated as cold war enemy installations; we subsequently prepared Intelligence Reports (IRs) on what we observed.

Our final fieldwork exam was an intelligence mission against the Baltimore dock area; our "enemies" were students in the Fort Holobird Army Counter Intelligence School. They were given a description of the car we were driving so we knew we would be spotted on arrival. I hatched a plan to foil theirs. We used my beat-up old Ford and stuffed bicycles into the trunk. We parked the car a good distance from the port and went in on the bikes. To be sure I would be seen immediately if I went in first, I wore an outlandish outfit topped with a red hunting cap. I was spotted instantly – but the others got in undetected, took photos of the dock area, and got out cleanly. It was a great coup for the Navy!

The topic I chose for my research paper was right-wing extremism, a popular subject in 1961. I did research both at the Library of Congress and at the headquarters of the Anti-Defamation League, where I was given access to unpublished material. I got an A+ on the paper, an amazing grade as my professor, Dr. Kalish, was a very conservative Republican. (Some years later Commander Sam Pearlman, who was ultimately promoted to Captain, plagiarized my paper and submitted it at the Naval War College in Newport, Rhode Island.)

Finally, as a graduation exercise, the whole class was divided into task groups to create an Intelligence Annex and Operational Plan based on a hypothetical situation. We were told to postulate that the Soviet Union had placed intermediate range ballistic missiles in Cuba, creating an existential threat to the United States. The plan we came up with was to establish what is known as a pacific ("peaceful") blockade, technically an act of war, concluding that the Soviets would back down. Two years later, when the hypothetical became the reality known as the Cuban Missile Crisis, our plan was forwarded to the Commander of the U.S. Atlantic Fleet (CINCLANTFLT), and formed the basis for planning the actual naval blockade which led to Soviet withdrawal of the missiles.

A mini-course in counterinsurgency was added to the curriculum of NIS by order of President Kennedy, who was just beginning to deal with issues in Southeast Asia. It was directed that on completion of this course a letter of qualification would be placed in our service records. Little did I know that this would have a highly significant effect on a future assignment.

As we approached graduation I applied for the job of Assistant Naval Attaché to Israel. Unfortunately, at the time, they could not send a Jewish officer to that job, but not out of any anti-Semitic bias. The reason was that all attachés have a secondary country to visit and Israel's secondary country was Egypt, at the time off-limits for Jews. So my good friend and carpool mate, Howard Burdick, a staunch New England Congregationalist, got the job. He loved Israel so much that when his son was born there he named him Joshua.

I was very pleased to be ordered, upon NIS graduation, to the Naval Scientific and Technical Intelligence Center (NAVSTIC), located at the Naval Observatory in Washington, for a two-year tour of shore duty.

CHAPTER EIGHT

★ ★ ★

Stateside Shore Duty

PART 2

THE NONDESCRIPT weathered concrete building on the grounds of the Naval Observatory, then home to Admiral's House, the official quarters of the Chief of Naval Operations and now the residence of the Vice President of the United States, looked like nothing more than a high-security dungeon for political prisoners. That it was the Navy's primary finished intelligence production facility, housing a strange assortment of pipe-smoking (the women, also) scientists and technicians, was not at all apparent to outsiders. Still a lieutenant, I was assigned to the Navy Scientific and Technical Intelligence Center (STIC). I reported to the commander in charge of STIC 1E, the electronics unit, charged with the analysis of world shipboard electronics and the production of materials for use by Fleet operators, ashore and afloat.

Within a couple of weeks after I reported aboard, my commander retired. I was notified that since I was soon likely to be promoted to Lieutenant Commander, the unit was mine. I was STIC 1E. It was time to take a good look at what I commanded.

The leading civilian was a GS-15, equivalent to a Rear Admiral lower half. W. E. W. "Bill" Howe was a grey-haired Yale graduate with a background in electronics and a close working relationship with the Naval Research Laboratories as well as with his opposite numbers in Great Britain and Canada (making up what was called the CANUKUS Community), sharing intelligence at a very high level. Bill Howe would never admit that he was working for a lowly lieutenant, and introduced me to his colleagues at Army, Air Force Intelligence and at CIA as "Commander" Sacks. Since we wore civilian clothes every day except "payday" Friday (to show the civilians where their salaries came from), he could get away with it.

There were two GS-12 civilians (equal to field grade, i.e., Lieutenant Commander).

E. Smith was actually Ethel Smith, who analyzed all the electronic intelligence (ELINT) received from the fleet and sent appropriate feedback. For decades, hundred of shipboard ELINT specialists never knew that E. Smith, a legend by the early 1960s, was a woman.

Ethel edited one of our main publications, ATP 26-21, the electronic countermeasures publication I first used aboard USS *Des Moines* in 1956.

"Robbie" Robertson, also GS-12, was a taciturn WWII veteran and member of the Society of the Cincinnati, which required members to be a blood descendant of an officer in the American Revolutionary War. (Robertson reminded me of the fictional Perry Mason's intrepid investigator, Paul Drake, who was always able to call on information from a colleague in another agency.) Robbie's area of expertise was merchant marine radars.

Ivah Arnold, a grandmotherly lady, edited and helped put together several recognition publications which were updated annually.

Lt. Paul Thorpe, a wonderful up-from-the-ranks officer (termed "Mustang" in the Navy), had been an electronics technician aboard the USS *Nautilus* when it made its historic submerged cruise to the North Pole. (The classic message sent was "Nautilus 90 North.") Paul went to college under the Navy Enlisted Scientific Education Program (NESEP), receiving a commission, and ultimately went on to achieve the rank of Commander in the Navy. He was a key analyst of photography and ELINT sent by the general fleet units and by the ultra-secret (at the time) submarine reconnaissance missions.

SHORTLY AFTER I TOOK OVER the unit, Bill Howe left for six months at the National War College. His absence and the Cuban Missile Crisis plunged me into the middle of all the intelligence committees in which he was involved. But first, a brief look at the national intelligence organization as it was in 1962.

The reorganization of the national security organization under President Truman in 1947 established the Central Intelligence Agency (CIA) as the kingpin of the intelligence community. The CIA was charged with responsibility for foreign intelligence while the FBI was responsible for domestic intelligence. Also created at this time was the Department of Defense, replacing the old War Department of WWII.

The Director of Central Intelligence chaired the United States Intelligence Board (USIB), on which sat the Army Chief of Staff, Intelligence (ACSI), the Director of Naval Intelligence (DNI), the Director of Air Force Intelligence (DAFI), the FBI, the State Department, Treasury, and one or two others.

USIB had several committees, among which were the Economic Intelligence Committee (EIC), the Scientific Intelligence Committee (SIC), and the Committee on Overhead Reconnaissance (COMOR). The SIC had a major subcommittee for Electronics (SICELSubCom) and the EIC had one for Telecommunications and Electronics. Bill Howe was the Navy member of these two committees, and in his absence I was elevated into the heady circle of very senior civilian and military representatives of all the USIB members of these sub-committees that met monthly at CIA headquarters in Langley, Virginia. More on this later.

Suffice it to say that I had entered a world where TOP SECRET was mundane; everything was compartmented into special intelligence clearances that were like alphabet soup – a letter or codeword for each individual project, with caveats almost as restrictive as "Burn after (or before) reading."

A FEW ANECDOTES about my tour at STIC:

When the Cuban Missile Crisis bubbled over, it was our shop that had provided the fleet with the electronic emission characteristics of the Soviet radars in the surface-to-air missile sites protecting the nuclear missiles being installed in Cuba. Some of this ELINT had been obtained by airborne reconnaissance (U2 or USAF RB-47H or Navy Recce aircraft), some by submarine offshore collection, and, eventually, some by satellite collection. NATO assigned identifying names to the radars. For example, we knew that the acquisition radar for a SAM-3 site was the SPOONREST and the missile guidance radar was the FANSONG. Provided with the characteristics of these radars. our reconnaissance flights over Cuba were able to detect the signals as well as photograph the sites themselves. The signal information was provided by our shop to such projects as the SHRIKE program, creating an anti-radiation missile (ARM) being developed at the Naval Ordinance Test Center in China Lake, California. (*Some of this will play a role in Chapter 8.*)

One afternoon the phone rang and my secretary, Miss Jeanette Rezak, a beautiful young woman who had been the runner-up for Miss Minnesota in 1961, but more importantly was the best typist in the building, advised me that the Pentagon had called. Our *expert* on Soviet guided missile patrol boats (*Komar*-class), stationed in Cuban waters, was to be at the War Room at 5 PM to brief the Secretary of the Navy, the Chief of Naval Operations (CNO), and assorted admirals and generals on the characteristics of this vessel. WOW! Bill Howe was at school; Robbie Robertson and Paul Thorpe were off on a mission, and I had won the brass ring. Ivah Arnold saved the day. From our publication on ships and aircraft of the Soviet Fleet (ONI 21-7, I think) she copied the one-page list of characteristics we had, and two photos of the KOMAR were converted into briefing slides. (This was the class of patrol boat that fired the STYX missile, thus sinking an Israeli destroyer in 1957, and Cuba had about a dozen of them.) I was still quite nervous. Ivah said, "Remember, when you get in front of that gang, you will know more about the subject than anyone in the room." I remembered, and gave my three-minute briefing with confidence, receiving thanks from Admiral George Anderson, CNO. His aide sent a note to my skipper complimenting me.

Early on in my tour at STIC, President Kennedy expressed his dissatisfaction with national intelligence estimates filled with footnoted exceptions from the various military service intelligence chiefs. Thus, the Defense Intelligence Agency (DIA) was created and a power struggle ensued between the two behemoth agencies. As the Navy member of the Telecommunications and Electronics Subcommittee of EIC, I viewed the struggle for chairmanship with some glee. Finally, as the representative of the smallest member I, half with tongue in cheek, offered to take the chairmanship for a year until things sorted themselves out. By now I had been promoted to Lieutenant Commander and the high-ranking civilians could legitimately address me as Commander. Inasmuch as I was no threat to anyone or any agency, I was made chairman.

Ultimately, this resulted in preparing and delivering a technical paper on communications and electronics aboard Baltic Sea naval forces (i.e., Polish and East German). The venue was at the headquarters of Supreme Allied Commander, Europe,

DEPARTMENT OF THE ARMY
OFFICE OF THE ASSISTANT CHIEF OF STAFF FOR INTELLIGENCE
WASHINGTON, D.C. 20310

1 2 AUG 1965

ACSI-SA

SUBJECT: Letter of Commendation, Lt Commander Harold H. Sacks

TO: Bureau of Naval Personnel
        Arlington Annex
        Columbia Pike and Arlington Ridge Road
        Arlington, Virginia 20370

1. It has been my privilege to know Cmdr Sacks on two successive tours of his naval service.

2. For about three years I was very closely associated with Cmdr Sacks when we worked at the Scientific and Technical Intelligence Center. His competence as an administrator, as a contributor to technical intelligence, as a briefer and as a writer was outstanding. He was of tremendous assistance to me, most selflessly protecting me endlessly from excessive non-scientific burdens permitting me the most productive period of my intelligence career. He also maintained excellent leadership and continuity in the office soon after my arrival when I was detailed to the National War College.

3. His more recent duty at J-2, MACV in Saigon was also in an area of great interest to me in my present position. In my opinion he made an excellent contribution to our intelligence posture in this critical theater under difficult conditions. He demonstrated ability again to deal with foreign nationals and many military seniors with great success.

4. His recent debriefings, which were generously given on his leave time, were of great utility to the entire Department of the Army staff and to the National Security Agency. Significant action was generated by his well-expressed suggestions.

ACSI-SA
SUBJECT: Letter of Commendation, Lt Commander Harold H. Sacks

5. Cmdr Sacks is the type of aggressive, competent officer
that all services need to retain. It is sincerely hoped that
he will be given favorable consideration at the time of his next
promotion review and that this letter will be inserted in his
appropriate file.

W. E. W. HOWE
Senior Scientific Advisor

DEPARTMENT OF THE NAVY
OFFICE OF THE CHIEF OF NAVAL OPERATIONS
WASHINGTON 25. D. C.

IN REPLY REFER TO

4 JUN 1964

CONFIDENTIAL

CONFIDENTIAL - Unclassified when enclosure (1) is removed

From: Director of Naval Intelligence
To: LCDR Harold H. SACKS
Via: Officer-in-charge, Scientific and Technical Intelligence Center

Subj: Performance of Duty

Encl: (1) Chairman, Economic Intelligence Committee, USIB,
           memorandum of 27 May 1964; subj: Commendation for
           LCDR Harold H. SACKS

1. Enclosure (1) is delivered to you with pride and my heartiest
congratulations.

2. In addition to noting the substantive contribution which you
have made to U.S. national intelligence, I would like to express
my personal appreciation for the manner in which you have represented naval intelligence on this inter-agency committee. The
competency of our representation on inter-agency boards and
committees controls the degree of respect and confidence in which
naval intelligence is held by the intelligence community, and you
have performed to the highest standards in this regard.

3. While the classification of enclosure (1) precludes its
appendage to your report of fitness, a copy of this letter will
be so appended. To this purpose, the following quotation from
enclosure (1) is made:

> "After having served as a member of the Subcommittee since
> December 1962, LCDR SACKS was appointed Chairman on 7
> January 1964. He has provided the Subcommittee with
> dynamic leadership and has worked unceasingly to make
> it a more meaningful force within the intelligence
> community. The broadening scope of Subcommittee activi-
> ties in recent months is due, in large measure, to his
> stimulating leadership."

RUFUS L. TAYLOR

CONFIDENTIAL
CONFIDENTIAL

where the first high-level British/German/American intelligence conference was held. I also visited some of STIC's human assets in Frankfurt and Wiesbaden. We would send our representative to various trade fairs such as the Levantine Trade Fair in Bari, on the Adriatic coast of Italy. There it was possible to purchase, for example, a Soviet-made television set. We would ship that to the CIA laboratory run by my colleague Chuck Pecci, who would tear it down completely. Knowing that the technology in the set, the power supply, transistors, relays, switches, etc., were about five years behind Soviet military technology, we could by interpolation come up with pretty good assumptions concerning current Soviet missile guidance technology. (This is how so much technical intelligence became known as the "digging of potatoes and spreading of manure.")

Bill Howe returned from the National War College and was very pleased with my administration of the unit. He said that he had been accustomed to unit heads who were waiting out their days until retirement, and appreciated my relieving him of administrative duties and freeing him up for research and analysis. He then went on a creative binge, producing very rough drafts of tremendously insightful technical reports on Soviet submarines and missiles, derived from highly classified U.S. submarine surveillance operations. My job was to edit them and see them through to publication. Bill went on to become the senior civilian technical intelligence advisor to the U.S. Army Chief of Staff, Intelligence (ACSI).

It was exciting to be in Washington during the "Camelot" days of the Kennedy administration. Annabel and I were invited to numerous embassies for cocktails. At the French embassy she made a great entrance, knocking over a huge receptacle for cigarette butts. At the British embassy we were greeted by Lord Ormsby-Gore whose glamorous wife was seen often with

Jackie Kennedy. Asked by an equerry what she wanted to drink, Annabel, without thinking, replied, "Vodka tonic please."

"Wrong embassy," the equerry replied.

"Oh, gin! I meant gin, gin and tonic," she answered, blushing deeply.

AN INTERESTING SIDEBAR involves Nicholas "Nicky" Shadrin, a Soviet defector working as a translator in the scientific branch of STIC. Although he couldn't get a security clearance, there were reams of unclassified documents in Russian, Polish and German which had to be mined for clues as to Iron Curtain scientific development. Nicky, I learned, had been a Destroyer Escort (DE) skipper and escaped with his wife Blanka, arriving in the U.S. via Sweden in 1959. Extensively debriefed for his valuable knowledge of Soviet bloc naval forces, equipment and tactics, he spent five years at STIC until made a U.S. citizen by a special act of Congress. Nicky became a consultant to the DIA and in 1966 was approached by the KGB and asked to work for the Soviets. With FBI approval he became a double agent and subsequently departed for Vienna in 1975 with material to give to the KGB. Nicky left his hotel to meet with KGB agents Mikhail Kuryshev and Oleg Kozlov and was never heard from again. Blanka Shadrin and friends enlisted the help of Henry Kissinger, President Gerald Ford, Zbigniew Brzezinski and numerous U.S. senators and congressmen. Friends wrote; all to no avail. Cold War considerations made it unlikely that the U.S. government would mount a major effort to save Nicky.

WE WERE INVOLVED IN the Oxon Hill Players, a little theater group that won the National One-Act Play Competition in 1964, and I taught Freshman English for one year at George Washington University, one evening a week. Annabel became

DEPARTMENT OF STATE

Washington, D.C. 20520

September 15, 1977

Comm. Harold H. Sacks
305 Porter Island Road
Virginia Beach, Virginia 23456

Dear Commander Sacks:

On behalf of President Carter, I want to thank you for your letter concerning Mr. Nicholas Shadrin. We appreciate your concern for Mr. Shadrin's welfare.

The Department became aware of Mr. Shadrin's case when we learned of his disappearance in Vienna and our efforts since then have been directed toward locating him and having him returned to his family and friends. These efforts are continuing.

Sincerely,

Hodding Carter III
Assistant Secretary
for Public Affairs and
Department Spokesman

DEPARTMENT OF DEFENSE
DEFENSE INTELLIGENCE SCHOOL
U. S. NAVAL STATION
WASHINGTON 25, D. C.

U- 31247/T1

27 NOV 1963

SUBJECT: Letter of Appreciation

TO: Officer in Charge
         U.S. Naval Scientific and Technical Intelligence Center
         Washington, D.C. 20390

1. On 20 November 1963, Lcdr H. H. Sacks, USN, assisted by Lt G.
Coacley, USN, and Messrs. N. Crozier and R. Winters, addressed the
Defense Intelligence Course, Class 1-64, on the subject, "Soviet
Early Warning." This most complex topic was presented expertly and
graphically, and conveyed knowledge of great value to the student
body.

2. On behalf of the faculty and students of the Defense Intelligence
Course, I wish to express my sincere thanks to you for making the
address possible. Please convey my appreciation to Lcdr Sacks and
his colleagues for their valuable contribution to the effectiveness
of the curriculum.

FOR THE COMMANDANT:

JOHN A. WIEGARD
Commander, USN
Executive Officer

involved with Children's Theater and served on the board of the National Children's Theater, which resulted in an invitation to the home of the President's Scientific Advisor, Dr. Wisner, where we met and had time to chat with Ethel Kennedy.

But my training in counterinsurgency at the Naval Intelligence School, which was now the Defense Intelligence School, paid off in a scary way: I received orders to the U.S. Military Assistance Command, Vietnam (USMACV) to report in July 1964. Our family had to come to grips with the prospect of a year-long separation.

CHAPTER NINE

★ ★ ★

365 Days and a Wake-Up

PART 1

IN EARLY SUMMER of 1964 there were about 13,000 U.S. military personnel in the Republic of Vietnam. On June 20, a young and vibrant commander, Lt. General William Westmoreland, pinned on his fourth star, relieved General Paul Harkins, and the U.S. Military Assistance Group (USMAG) became the U.S. Military Assistance Command Vietnam (USMACV). I was ordered to report for duty under the Chief of Staff (COSI), Intelligence (J2). (That Counterinsurgency course at PG school may have been the culprit.) Annabel and I were faced with a choice: one year unaccompanied by family or two years accompanied.

Smiling on the day of departure

Fortunately, as it turned out, we elected to unaccompanied, for "365 days and a wake-up."

My departure was preceded by a round of farewell celebrations from various groups in the intelligence community with which I had worked. One of the Deputy Directors of CIA thought I should not go to Vietnam, and offered to arrange my transfer out of the Navy to a higher paid position at the Central Intelligence Agency (CIA). Faced with twelve months away from my family, I found the offer very tempting; however, I still had my heart set on one day commanding a destroyer.

I flew commercial air to San Francisco, shuttled to Travis Air Force Base, checked in and the next morning arrived at the departure terminal. We were issued boarding passes and proceeded to the tarmac, only to learn that our flights had been delayed 24 hours. The good news was that by being officially "boarded" the day counted as "day one" of duty. I was now faced with only 364 days and a wakeup.

Arrival at Ton Son Nhut airport provided the first indication that I was entering a war zone. Unable to make the kind of long gradual descent typical at commercial fields, our DC-8 behaved like a dive bomber in order to reduce its vulnerability to Viet Cong small arms fire, making a steep screaming approach and leveling off just in time to land. Upon landing, we were processed into a large briefing room and, tired as we were from our twenty-hour trip, our spirits could not have been higher when General Westmoreland – himself – entered as our briefing officer. (There were so few American troops arriving in 1964 that he met each flight personally.) He handed each of us a U.S. Expeditionary Force medal, and made it clear that what had until then been a typical "counterinsurgency effort" was expected to escalate dramatically in the coming months. We were in for an exciting year. Ironically, we were also handed tourist literature advertising tiger hunting in the highlands, water-skiing in the Na Bhe River, and sunbathing on the beaches of Phuoc Tuy Province.

After a week of intensive orientation, during which I shared a suite at the aged Majestic Hotel with six field-grade army officers, and during which the USS *Maddox* (DD 731) was attacked by North Vietnamese patrol torpedo boats, we received our assignments. I reported to Army Colonel Ben Ward, Chief of the Production Branch, J2, and was further assigned as provincial analyst for Go Cong and Phuc Tuoy Provinces under the supervision of LCol Peter Uiberall.

General Westmoreland

Pete Uiberall was a fascinating person: a Viennese Jew who just made it out of Austria in 1938 as a kid, he served as an interpreter at the Nuremburg war trials and later came to Vietnam as an interpreter for General Harkins, General Westmoreland's predecessor. Pete was fluent in French and all official meetings between Harkins and Premier Diem (ultimately assassinated – allegedly with tacit CIA approval) took place in French. I was privileged to read his translator's notes of these conversations and one sticks in my head. Harkins, in September of 1963, says to Diem, "Well, it looks like we will be finished here and home for Christmas." Diem replies, "I and my family have been governing provinces and the country for two generations. I can tell you that you are mistaken if you think this will end in even ten years." How prescient was that?

My task was to collect and review all intelligence reports from various sources in my area of interest. They were from U.S. Intelligence advisors, Army of the Republic of Vietnam (ARVN) sources, defector interviews, prisoner of war interrogations – from wherever information came. I would produce, by Saturday, a weekly summary to be collated with summaries from other intelligence analysts, which would be further collated with summaries from a myriad of operations analysts in the J3, which would finally, by Sunday night, be sent to the Chairman of the Joint Chiefs of Staff as the Weekly Military Report (MILREP) of the USMACV. The report would be further massaged on Monday in Washington for the weekly Tuesday meeting of the National Security team.

My report was mostly boilerplate. It would read, in part, something like this:

During the period 11-18 September there were 17 firefights, 11 incidences of sabotage, 2 assassinations, 3 kidnappings and 17 other incidences of violence. According to reliable reports the Viet Cong, operating at night, executed a village chief, and collected taxes. The reduction of such incidences from the previous report indicates some success in the pacification of the area.

EXAMINED IN THE COLD LIGHT of day, it is more likely that the reduction of "incidences" was due to a lazy ARVN company commander remaining in his fortified position at night, without conducting active patrols and ambushes. With little opposition the VC were free to operate, thereby negating the need for a great deal of armed conflict. In areas where the commander was ordering active patrols and setting ambushes, there was interruption of VC activity leading to more firefights and the wrong conclusion that there was less pacification.

I was not a happy camper. Here I was on a joint staff made up of "top ten-percenters," each of us making a personal sacrifice to be there, and I resented being relegated to a mundane "bean counting" job. But – there were some high notes. One was my meeting and befriending Major Steve Samuels, a Jewish army operator in our branch. My security clearances from STIC precluded my leaving Saigon. Steve traveled widely in my area of interest and from him I could get real information, real-time. I had purchased a motorbike to get to and from my quarters in a spartan hotel just built in Cholon, the Chinese quarter of Saigon, on the end of a long thoroughfare called Tranh Hung Dao. The armored buses were safer than a motorbike but stifling hot.

Hal on his 50cc Ischia motorbike in front of the Hotel Continental of "Ugly American" Fame.

Steve and I would meet after work and ride off to dinner; he was about Skip's height and weight (as an adult) and perched well on the back of my motorbike. We made a great professional team for a few months, until an unusual chain of events catapulted me into a high-visibility analytical job.

Because my assignment took about twenty percent of my time and our workday was twelve hours day, seven days a week, when a requirement came down from General Stillwell, Chief of Staff for USMACV, for a study of Vietnamese political parties, I was asked to take it on. I motored over to the American Embassy to speak with the political experts there, including the CIA agents. During the course of my several visits to read their files I was introduced to Deputy Ambassador U. Alexis Johnson, a brilliant career State Department professional who subsequently served as

Undersecretary of State and was the chief delegate to the SALT talks of the early 1970s. Ambassador Johnson was sent to Saigon to keep Ambassador Maxwell Taylor ("The Too Uncertain Trumpet") from treating the sensitive and volatile Vietnamese generals like schoolboys. He was kind enough to give me some personal insights into the political parties in Vietnam, some of which were merely "tea-drinking" societies, and remembered me months later when, following the bombing of the U.S. Embassy, he set up his office next to mine at our headquarters on Rue de Pasteur.

I completed my study, and one of my conclusions was that, in addition to the Cao Dai Party, attention need be paid to the militant Buddhist monks who had great influence among the populace and the enlisted men of the ARVN (eighty percent of enlisted men were Buddhist while eighty percent of the officers were Catholic). Before the study could advance to the Chief of Staff, I needed the concurrence of two other Js: the J3 (Ops) and the J5 (Plans). My true introduction to the intricacies of joint staff procedures came at this time. The journey of a study through the Navy chain of command was perilous enough; on the joint staff it was positively serpentine. Each level that needed to "initial" the study looked less into the content and more for any hidden threat to their organization. I began walking my study, now attached to a paper called a distribution form (DF), through the staff layers.

Perhaps because so little was known about Vietnamese political parties, each level within the J5 wanted to actually read the study before chopping on it. Thus, I spent two days waiting in outer offices until finally Major General Adams, the J5, shook my hand and signed off. The same was true for the J3; Major General William "Bill" DePuy not only read it but called me for a thirty-minute discussion of my sources and then wanted to know what the hell a destroyer officer was doing on this staff. We had coffee and, although he was always "General" to me, for the rest of the year I was "Hal" to him. (When I eventually got to my new role he was very attentive to my briefings – but that is for the next chapter.) DePuy was 45 years old when we met. He had been a company and battalion commander during WWII, fighting his way across Europe. After his tour as J3 he commanded the 1st Army Division ("the Big Red One") and as a four-star general in later years developed the post-Vietnam training doctrine for the Army, which was the basic doctrine in use for decades until rewritten by General Petraeus over 30 years later.

One day, a month or so after I reported aboard, I received a phone call from the Adjutant General's office. "Sacks, you're Jewish, aren't you?" "Yes," I replied. "Well, it might interest you to know that a helicopter is inbound with what will likely be the first Jewish fatality in Nam." I rushed down to my motorbike and tore off to the Naval Hospital in Cholon. There on the steps of the hospital, waiting for the chopper, was the head surgeon, a Jewish commander, and the head nurse, also a Jewish commander. The chopper landed and the soldier was stretchered off. He never made it into surgery.

I headed back to my office and called the Adjutant's office to find out the name and whereabouts of the nearest Jewish Chaplain. "There is no Jewish Chaplain in Nam," he advised.

There I was again, apparently the senior-involved-Jew-in-the-neighborhood (which turned out to be wrong; there was a Jewish Army LCOL with whom I became friends later on). I checked the roster because I heard that there a Jewish general in-country. Once again, the Adjutant's officer advised that the logistics commander, Major General Brown, was "rumored" to be Jewish but he was "out in the compound off Tranh Hung Dai." After the morning briefing I called for an appointment. His orderly asked what I needed to see him about. "It's a Jewish matter," I replied. Silence. Then after a few minutes, "The general will see you at 1100 hours."

General Brown had a pained expression on his face. He looked like someone called up for an *aliyah* (the honor of participating in the Torah reading) but who had forgotten the *brochot* (the blessings). I introduced myself and expressed my concern that there was no Jewish chaplain in-country and that my research (based on a quick search for Jewish-sounding surnames) indicated there were 150-200 Jewish personnel and that we were

beginning to take casualties. "I'm not a practicing Jew," Brown said. As soon as I replied, "It doesn't take any practice, General," I feared I had crossed a line. Brown visibly reddened, appeared to think for a moment, and quietly asked, "What do you want me to do, Commander Sacks?" I answered, "Get us a chaplain, please."

LCol Meir Engel

And he did! Not too many rabbis were anxious to come to Vietnam, but LCol Meir Engel, 54 years old, arrived a few weeks later from Fort Ord, California. He was a dynamic man and immediately set out to visit and counsel Jewish personnel around the country, returning from his helicopter, jeep, and patrol boat trips in time for Friday night services. I became the official Jewish lay leader.

TWO THINGS CHANGED my life in Vietnam. First, I was able to talk my way out of the distant hotel in which I was first quartered to the Rex Hotel in downtown Saigon, much closer to MACV headquarters. I occupied a suite with an Army major who was away all the time but, more importantly, the quarters were adjacent to the modest Jewish chapel we established. Friday night services became a weekly ritual, followed by either an *Oneg Shabbat* in the chapel or an Asian dinner at a floating Chinese restaurant – about a ten-minute walk. Scheduling of the *Onegs* depended on receipt of a monthly shipment of New York bagels courtesy of my father-in-law, Nat Glicksman. He would double-wrap and freeze each bagel individually and ship them via Fleet Post Office (FPO) New York. They would arrive about a week later, defrosted but fresh. I would purchase canned salmon and cream cheese at the commissary and it was amazing to see the surprise on the faces of kids just in from the field with automatic rifles, grenades and full combat rig when they saw bagels in Saigon. Our congregation grew beyond the military as the Economic Counsel of the British Embassy showed up with his family (and eventually hosted a couple of great *Shabbat* dinners at his villa) and an Israeli businessman and his Vietnamese wife (sporting a large Star of David) joined us as well.

Nat was very interested in what I was doing and we exchanged reel-to-reel taped messages weekly. He never recorded over my tapes; he replaced them with fresh tape and spliced my correspondence onto large reels. I still have them but haven't yet attempted to listen to them.

Frequently after the services, we walked the five or six blocks from the hotel to a floating Chinese restaurant. One Friday night our services were a bit longer (perhaps it was *Rosh Hodesh*, a new month) and we set off for the restaurant several minutes later than usual. Halfway there we heard a loud explosion. Arriving at the restaurant we were greeted by a grisly scene. A Claymore mine had been detonated on the gangway leading to the restaurant, killing and injuring many diners. Had we not been delayed by the longer service, we all might have been among the casualties.

THE SECOND LIFE-CHANGING event will be covered in the next chapter.

COMMANDER, U. S. NAVAL BASE
GUANTANAMO BAY, CUBA
10 November 1964

MAIL ADDRESS:
BOX 34, NAVY NO. 115
FPO, NEW YORK, N. Y.

Lieutenant Commander Harold H. SACKS, USN
HQ MACV (J-2)
APO 143, San Francisco

Admiral Sacks, Sir:

In reply to your letter as to the goings on around
here I think that the enclosed summary of the military
situation is best to give you an idea of what is going on.

Basically the Cubans are preparing to reenforce. The
order of battle against us here is 15,000 troops, 150 tanks
and 300 artillery pieces.

We have a thin red line as usual with our backs to
the sea. We are capable of being reenforced by air and
by sea. Our two airfields could be denied us by light
artillery as well as mortar fire.

We are constantly pinged at by the Cubans but no
indications that it is a deliberate government order. Just
irresponsible acts on the part of the individual soldier.

All else well - and your letter was most interesting
and gave me a good idea of your area.

I knew General Westmoreland. How is he doing?

Warmest regards to you and Annabelle,

JOHN D. BULKELEY
Rear Admiral, U. S. Navy

CHAPTER TEN

★ ★ ★

365 Days and a Wake-Up

PART 2

HAVING WORKED in technical intelligence during my previous tour I was naturally curious to learn about the tech-intel operation at MACV. To my dismay I learned that the tech-intel officer was an army warrant officer, skilled in the recognition of various types of firearms. I asked if there was any concern that the Viet Cong, still considered to be a rag-tag bunch of black-pajama'd guerrillas, might at some point demonstrate greater sophistication. All I got was a shrug. Recalling that there had been, until recently, a Naval Attaché, I inquired after the Navy publications, many of which had been produced by my office at STIC. "There are some piles of books stashed in the General's latrine. You might look there," I was told by a senior marine sergeant. Sure enough, I found all the electronics pubs I had nursed into production.

The next day I inquired if there were any routine but classified messages from the Pacific Command (PACOM) Headquarters covering the subject of Electronic Intelligence (ELINT). Yes, there were, but nobody read them. I asked that they be routed to me. Thus I began to scan the PACOM ELINT reports, which summarized the signals collected by a variety of airborne, ship-borne, and land-based platforms. Not scintillating reading – line after line of frequency, pulse width and related data

– I was nevertheless astonished to read of an intercept in North Vietnam of a radar NATO-designated SPOONREST, which I knew from the days of the Cuban missile crisis was the "putter-on" radar for the Soviet SA-3 surface-to-air missile launcher. Experience told me it would be just a matter of time until the guidance radar for the missile, designated FANSONG, would be detected.

Every evening at 5PM there was a MACV briefing attended by senior officers. Majors and Lcdrs were like messenger boys on such a top-heavy staff. We were told to stand at the back and keep our mouths shut. The briefing officer, usually a Colonel, would end the briefing with, "Are there any questions?" Westmoreland or one or more of the two-star generals would ask a question, but this afternoon I had the temerity to ask, "What are we doing about the SAM sites being built in North Vietnam?" The briefer indicated that they had no knowledge of that and the briefing was ended. General Carl Youngdale, the J2, glared at me and ordered me to his office. He asked me what the hell I thought I was doing and what did I know about it anyway. I explained my rationale to him and he asked if I had the intercept messages to prove it. I said I did. He then

General Carl Youngdale, USMC

called down to the office of Major General Stillwell, the Chief of Staff, and asked if he could be seen. Then he told me to gather up my stuff and meet him at the Chief's office in five minutes.

Major General Richard G. Stillwell had been Commandant of Cadets at West Point when General Westmoreland was Superintendent of the Military Academy, and was brought in to be Chief of Staff to his old boss. He went on to command the U.S. Military Assistance Command, Thailand, the 1st Armored Division, and U.S. Forces in Korea. He retired as a four-star general and served as Undersecretary of Defense.

"Chief," General Youngdale said, "This is LCdr Sacks, who works in my shop."

"Sacks?" Stillwell replied, "Just what in hell are you talking about?" I placed a sheaf of SECRET ELINT reports from PACOM on his desk and pointed to where I had underlined the frequency of the SPOONREST radar. Then I showed him the photo of the radar in my ONI publication, along with photos of a finished missile site. Then I told him that we might expect an intercept of the FANSONG missile guidance radar any day. He spent the next ten minutes asking me about my background, previous duty stations, experience, etc, and dismissed me with a cordial smile and a handshake. I saluted.

The next morning I was notified by Pete Uiberall that I was leaving his department and was promoted to Chief, Special Research Section, upstairs "behind the green door" in the Special Intelligence area.

And on the next morning we received notice from PACOM of an intercept of the FANSONG radar in North Vietnam.

General Youngdale came up to my new office, a large cubbyhole, congratulated me, introduced me around and told me that I was to exercise staff supervision over an Army airborne medium-frequency direction-finding program and assigned two National Security Agency (NSA) civilian analysts and an Air force Staff Sergeant to my Section. I was to bone up on the operation and be prepared for a briefing of the Js on Saturday morning at 8 AM, four days away.

THERE WAS A LOT TO LEARN, and the fact that General Westmoreland was getting ready to request a significant buildup of U.S. forces in Vietnam meant that new interest would be invested in some of the more esoteric intelligence we were beginning to gather. My NSA analysts briefed me on the state of communications intelligence. But we were basically unable to read their codes, not because of their sophistication but actually due to their primitive use of what is called a "one-time pad." In other words, each simple letter and number substitution code sheet was used only one time, thus frustrating our computer code-cracking capability, which depended upon repetition. What could be done, however, was to determine through high frequency direction-finding (HFDF) the general location of the originator of a message, and then using medium-range direction-finding (MRDF) techniques to determine within three to five kilometers the location of the recipient. Thus, hand-keyed continuous wave Morse code transmissions from the Hanoi area were ascribed to the Lao Dong Party Headquarters and subjected to traffic analysis. It was thus possible to create a chart of the Enemy Order of Battle (EOB) as one station would be answered by several stations under its control and each of those stations would speak to and be answered by several stations under *its* control. In other words, Divisional Headquarters in Hanoi issued orders to Regimental Headquarters in the field which in turn controlled Battalion Headquarters, and so on. We couldn't understand what they were saying, but could analyze the level of communications activity, and the approximate movement of subordinate units. Experienced cryptologists, such as were present in Vietnam at protected sites, could recognize the electronic signatures (the "fist") of individual operators.

THIS MAY SEEM rather dry, but is essential to understanding what we were able to accomplish in the coming months. The MRDF operation was run out of Ton Son Nhut airfield by a small group of intrepid army aviators flying single-engine and small twin-engine prop-type aircraft with a radio and DF operator embarked. The colonel in charge took me for a spin. Flying over the jungle and rivers at low altitude for the first time was an exhilarating and pretty scary experience. In time, and on other flights, it would still be exhilarating but a little less scary. I quickly learned the technique. First, the radio operator came up on the frequency he would expect communications on at a given time. Then, upon receipt the DF operator would establish a line of bearing to the transmitter. The pilot would then circle in order to get a triangulating fix, accurate, as I have said, between three and five kilometers. It all sounds so simple, but success depended upon superb airmanship flying at low altitudes and very vulnerable to small arms fire, and a radio operator steeped in signal recognition. My office would be receiving that afternoon the results of the collection efforts that day. Using the EOB information at hand I would learn that a regimental or battalion or company-size unit had moved from its position last week to a new position. Of course it was understood that we were not tracking the unit but its radio, which could be hidden several kilometers away from the unit itself. Up until now, the security surrounding communications intelligence prevented this information going anywhere, and there was no point in mounting an operation to catch two North Vietnamese Army (NVA) radiomen operating with a transmitter no larger than a picnic basket and a receiver concealed in a small lunch-size rice bucket.

Viet Cong (VC) battalions and regiments were locally manned but augmented by cadres from the north. These were usually officers and technical rates, such as radiomen, infiltrated through what was popularly called the Ho Chi Minh trail. The radiomen would enter southern cities and buy the components of radio transmitters and receivers at local hardware stores, and then build their own communication stations. Among the surveillance tools at MACV's disposal were overhead photography, both daylight and infrared, and side-looking radar (SLAR). Overhead photography was needed to see vertically through the triple-tier canopy of trees, and SLAR was able to be flown along a river or stream and seek images in the near range. Infrared was able to detect campfires. I was furnishing MRDF data to an army colonel on loan to MACV from the Central Intelligence Agency. He created a Targeting Research Analysis Center (TRAC), which overlaid information from at least three sources to create a target. So our fixes had one purpose, but it was my task to create another. Details later.

Saturday morning came and I wore my sharpest Navy tropical white uniform and had coffee ready for the assembled generals: Youngdale the J2, DePuy the J3, Milton Adams the J5 (Plans), a colonel in charge of the Current Intelligence Indications Center (my landlord), and finally Generals Westmoreland and Stilwell. Our briefing materials were primitive. I had large-scale charts of the Saigon-Gia

Preparing for MF/DF flight

Dinh district, each of the four separate Corps areas and one full-length chart of both North and South Vietnam, along with charts of Laos and Cambodia. They were mounted on eight-foot-tall sliding boards, each of which were about six feet wide, and my Air Force Sergeant knew when to roll out which boards.

I was given ten minutes to explain how the HFDF and MFDF operation worked and show some of the results. Following an intensive line of questioning, I was told to be prepared to brief twice weekly.

How could we use this information to warn our American advisors when an attack on their compound was imminent? We couldn't clear them for COMINT if they were to be deployed in areas where they could be captured. For the same reason I was not permitted to leave Saigon in a single-engine aircraft or in a helicopter unless there was a second helicopter in company. None of the gung ho army and marine officers was willing to be briefed in to intelligence that would interfere with their being with their troops in the field. I sent a proposal to General Stillwell via General Youngdale (no laborious use of the Army's DF system in Special Intelligence) suggesting that we brief senior advisors to be alert for, and take action on, a high priority message from "a reliable agent" indicating an imminent attack. Only General Westmoreland could originate a message from COMUSMACV, but General Stillwell could originate a message from USMACV.

After a few occasions where I was forced to have the General awakened during the night, I was given his permission to originate and release "immediate" messages such as:

"USMACV SENDS – A RELIABLE AGENT INDICATES POSSIBILITY OF ATTACK YOUR AREA BY ENEMY FORCES."

I was authorized to brief the advisors on the reliability of my reports and to make them understand that when they received one, it was time to get their heads down.

On the evening of January 9, 1965, a "reliable agent" report was sent by me to the commander of a Special Forces (SF) detachment that the VC 272 Infantry Regiment had taken position four kilometers north of the Thuan Loi rubber plantation in Phuoc Long Province. Put on alert, the detachment of eleven SF soldiers and nine Navy Seabees organized ARVN forces in time to successfully defend their position, causing the VC forces to withdraw with heavy casualties, and permitting our advisors to leave safely for our base in Bien Hoa.

A similar warning to the U.S. advisors at an ARVN post in Dong Xoi (three stations believed to support a VC regiment each had closed in over a few days) allowed the insertion of units of the 173rd Airborne Brigade which had arrived in May, and again, heavy losses were inflicted upon the VC regiments.

Up until this time we were dealing with VC units augmented by cadres of NVA soldiers.

One morning I was astonished to note a HFDF fix on a unit believed to be the communications HQ for the North Vietnamese 305th Infantry Division formerly stationed in Dong Hoi. Its appearance in Quang Tri, the northernmost province of South Vietnam, represented a quantum increase in North Vietnamese tactics. These were no black-pajama troops. They were jack-booted, heavily armed infantry, supported by heavy artillery (155mm howitzers) and armored personnel carriers. I called General Youngdale immediately. He took a couple of extra puffs on his pipe and asked me if I was certain. I called in my NSA linguist who had already double-checked the identification. I suggested we wait 12 hours to see if the unit was moving south or if it was just a tentative incursion to test the response. Youngdale agreed. The next fix was 10 kms. further south. We called Generals Stillwell and Westmoreland. A new phase of the war had begun. I was awarded the Joint Service Commendation Medal for this discovery.

ONE OTHER INSTANCE where technical intelligence led to important operational reaction involved our watching, over several months, the development of a network believed to be involved with maritime infiltration of supplies from the north. The standard mental picture of the dedicated VC courier, leaving the north with 60 pounds of rice and making his way down the jungle-covered Ho Chi Minh trail on his sandals made of cut-up rubber tires, consuming 15 pounds of rice and delivering 45 pounds, did not account for the resupply of hundreds of thousands of rounds of ammunition, grenades, Claymore mines and semiautomatic weapons and grenade launchers. Our traffic analysis indicated the control station in Hanoi was directing traffic to subordinate stations at sea. I spoke with Navy Captain Hardcastle, Chief of the Navy Military Assistance Group. He initially refused to be briefed in, not wishing to be hampered in his movements around the country. I prevailed on General Youngdale to order the Captain in for a somewhat sanitized briefing. It was agreed that upon receipt of a "reliable agent report" from USMACV, Captain Hardcastle would arrange for a recon mission.

FOR MERITORIOUS SERVICE . . . Commander Harold H. Sacks (right), commanding officer of the USS Steinaker (DD-863), was presented the Joint Service Commendation Medal for meritorious service while serving in Vietnam. The award was presented by Captain B. R. Eggeman, the former commander of Destroyer Squadron Two and now attached to the Office of the Chief of Naval Operations.

I was awarded the Joint Service Commendation Medal.

Late on February 15 my Air Force sergeant called me in to the headquarters. He had just posted the latest fix on what we believed was an infiltrating vessel in the vicinity of Vung Ro Bay, in central South Vietnam. I released the warning report to Captain Hardcastle, and the next morning a U.S. Army reconnaissance helo spotted what appeared to be a large steel-hulled ship perpendicular to the shore. Upon receipt of the sighting report, the Senior Advisor to the South Vietnamese set the wheels in motion for an attack by South Vietnamese A-1 Skyraiders that resulted in the ship being capsized and sunk. Subsequent strikes rendered the stacked stores on the beach useless, and within a couple of days, SVN Naval units landed troops and naval commandos which swept the defending VC from their defensive positions.

More importantly, it was revealed that over 100 tons of Chinese and Soviet-made war materiél, including over a million rounds of small arms ammunition and between three and four thousand rifles, and thousands of grenades, mortar rounds and explosives, had been offloaded.

We all felt ecstatic as the U.S. Navy, particularly Vice Admiral Blackburn, commander of the U.S. Seventh Fleet, and General Westmoreland were looking for proof that significant maritime infiltration was taking place. The Admiral complimented us and asked me, in front of his entourage, how this should be handled. I got kind of red in the face, being put on the spot in front of a Navy Vice Admiral, but replied that the Navy knew how to handle this task, but also that the South Vietnamese really needed a counterpart to our Coast Guard, to train them in coastal surveillance. From this event General Westmoreland and Vice Adm. Blackburn pressed for the organization of Operation Market Time, and the U.S. Coast Guard became a major player in the war zone, along with ships and aircraft of the Seventh Fleet. (*In a later chapter the reader will learn about USS* Steinaker's *role in Operation Market Time.*)

During this whole time I was not totally neglecting the need to "have a life." I had begun teaching English to Vietnamese students at Hoi Viet My, the Vietnamese-American Association, two evenings a week. Our normal work week at MACV HQ was 0700 to 1900 daily, seven days a week.

I joined fellow officers over several rounds of scotch after work (usually around 1900 or 2000). Chivas Regal was about

$2.00 a bottle. We then had dinner in a French, Chinese, or Indian restaurant. Lobster thermidor was also about $2.00. In the morning I usually arrived at the compound by 0600, bringing a bag of sweet rolls made by the bakery at the Rex Hotel. After the early briefings, around 1000, I would head downtown for breakfast where I became a favorite of the owner, who frequently ate with me – I with chopsticks, and he with knife and fork. During the lunch period I would skip lunch, proceed to the roof of the Rex where there was a pool, and have a swim and a 20-minute nap before heading back.

This was the routine, seven days a week, except on occasion, if things were really slow, I would take off on a Sunday at around 1500 or 1600 and visit the zoo or an orphanage. One

Ten-year-old girl from orphanage

particular orphanage that Steve and I would visit was run by the Catholic Church. We'd single out a couple of kids and take them shopping for clothing and to a restaurant for a good meal.

There was even a racetrack where clearly undersized horses were raced before a cheering crowd. I felt very un-comfortable and exposed in such a large crowd and never returned after one trip.

On one occasion, a few of us were invited water skiing aboard a State Department boat. I was never much of a water skier but the idea of pleasure boating on the Na Be River was wild; but on the day we went, we were treated to small-arms fire from the shore, and that apparently ended such excursions permanently.

Ironically, frustrated earlier by being restricted to Saigon, I was now able to travel extensively as escort to General Youngdale or one of the numerous visiting VIPs, military or civilian, who had to be "shown around the country." Exercising staff supervision over the airborne direction-finding program, I was able to accompany their crews on numerous flights.

One trip with General Youngdale stands out. Lt. General Victor "Brute" Krulak, a hugely decorated war hero with the reputation of being tough as nails, was then Commander Fleet Marine Corp, Pacific (COMFMFPAC). He was determined to build a landing strip at Chu Lai in order to bring in USMC close air support for his detachment of the Third Marine Division, recently landed at Da Nang and posted in Chu Lai to the south, in order to protect vital naval interests in the area, such as the special intelligence operation at Phu Bai. And he was determined to build it out of a newly designed series of solid interlocking aluminum panels, which replaced the old WWII springy steel web-like sections. He bet General Youngdale a case of Jack

Off to Chu Lai

Daniels Black Label whisky that he would get it built in 30 days. Well, after about 25 days Youngdale decided to fly up to Chu Lai to see for himself how it was going. "Grab your sidearm, Sacks, and come along," he ordered.

This little evolution required two helicopters, one of which was piloted by a Marine Colonel and one by a Marine Brigadier General. The one-hour flight was uneventful and, upon arrival at Chu Lai, we were given a tour of the nearly finished airstrip and of the surrounding defensive network. We then proceeded to one of the outlying strong points where a platoon of marines were having the noon meal in their tent. Youngdale lifted up the tent flap and was greeted by a handsome 22-year-old Marine second Lieutenant who sprang to his feet, saluted smartly and ran over to hug "Uncle Carl." Youngdale then introduced me to "Charlie" Krulak, Brute Krulak's 23-year-old son. We were invited to join the platoon at lunch ("C" Rations) when incoming mortar fire broke up the festivities. Youngdale had me scoot out to get the choppers ready to depart, as it wouldn't be politically correct for MACV staffers to be caught in a firefight. We took off as soon as the jeeps we were riding could make it to the landing pad. Charles Krulak went on to become a four-star general and served from 1995-1999 as Commandant of the U.S. Marine Corps.

AFTER ABOUT 7 MONTHS in-country I came to the head of the R&R list; five days of rest and rehabilitation (some in the military called it "rape and rampage"). I chose Hong Kong, and in due course boarded a chartered DC-8 jet for Hong Kong, where I was booked into a suite at the Hong Kong Hilton for $5 a night. I made the rounds of all the recommended jewelry stores, purchased jade bracelets, Mikimoto pearls, toured the area, had a burgundy tuxedo jacket made and ate in all the best restaurants. Three years later, all the spade work came in handy when Annabel joined me during my WESTPAC tour in *Steinaker*. We replicated the five days, and purchased more jewelry at the same store. More on that in another chapter.

The sudden death of our Chaplain, LCol. Engel, due to a heart attack, was a blow to our small Jewish community; however, a replacement arrived just in time to help me prepare for Passover. Once again, the Jewish Welfare Board had sent the necessary food and wine. Now all we had to do was get the men and women in from their scattered posts around the country and find a place for them to sleep in Saigon, already short of quarters.

But we managed and held the first Seder ever held by the

The First Military Seder in Vietnam, 1965

military in Vietnam, attended by about 100 soldiers, sailors, and marines.

NEAR THE END OF MY YEAR in Vietnam, General Westmoreland asked me if I would consider a six-month extension as we now had over 250,000 troops in country and more were on the way. He said I would be sent home for two weeks with my family and then return. I reluctantly agreed. The Navy had other thoughts on the matter. The Bureau of Naval Personnel opined that I needed to serve as executive officer in a destroyer in order to be promoted to Commander. It was a bit of irony that distinguished service in a war zone might disqualify me for promotion.

With regards and best wishes always to :

A Soldier Reports

Harold H. Sacks

Commander,
U.S. Navy (Ret.)
Vietnam 1964-65 - Off-Shore
1968
W.C. Westmoreland

4/3/76

I received orders to the USS *Gyatt* (DD712), homeported in Norfolk, Virginia, as executive officer and departed Saigon at the end of my year's duty. On the long flight, first to Hawaii, then to California, then to Baltimore, I had quite a bit of time to reflect. I was so happy to be heading home to my family, yet a part of me felt that I was abandoning my "shipmates" in Vietnam.

CHAPTER ELEVEN

★ ★ ★

Back to the *Real* Navy

ANNABEL AND MY PARENTS met me at the airport when I landed following a two-day trip home from Vietnam. After a year apart, Annabel and I eyed each other almost like strangers, and the coming weeks were not given to a relaxed homecoming.

We hustled down from the DC area to Norfolk to find a place to live. Buying our first home was an adventure – and a stressful one. Many of our contemporaries had been stuck with homes in the Norfolk area when they were transferred elsewhere,

World Traveler
Adventurer

Unassuming Hero
V. C. Killer

HAROLD H. SACKS, LCDR USN
Ship Driver — Temporarily Unemployed
Soldier of Fortune — Specializing in
Maritime Infiltration and Counterinsurgency
By Appointment Only
ANNOUNCES HIS RETURN
To Naval Affairs aboard the good ship
U.S.S. GYATT (DD 712)

Saigon, Republic of Vietnam

Norfolk, Virginia

The card was only partly in jest.

Me in my new MG after returning from Vietnam

and we had no reason to suspect that we would spend more than two years at sea. We compromised on a modest split-level house that Judy and Skippy thought was palatial (that is, they each had their own room). Sadly, (yes, Skippy cried) before moving we transported and released our two pet ducks ("Sweet" and "Sour") at a Washington, DC duck pond – only to discover that there was a lovely pond, full of ducks, less than a street away from our Norfolk house in Poplar Halls.

Traditionally, all pictures, curtains and bric-a-brac had to be in place within 24 hours of moving in as I invariably shipped out very soon after. True to form, I executed the first part of my orders by reporting to Key West, Florida, to the Prospective Commanding Officer/Executive Officer Course – another month away from home. Spending a few weeks in class and at leisure with a dozen or so officers heading to commands and XO tours was actually very beneficial. It gave me the chance to be updated on current fleet operations and administration after being away from those operations for four years. Additionally, I had the opportunity to reinsert myself mentally into the blue-water game.

I reported to *Gyatt* at the Norfolk Naval Shipyard in Portsmouth, Virginia in my newly purchased MG-B convertible. USS *Gyatt* (DD 712) was commissioned in 1945, having been

USS *Gyatt* (DD712) in 1965.
(Note the aft twin 5" gun mount has been removed)

built by the Federal Shipbuilding and Drydock Company of Newark, New Jersey, at a cost of just under $9 million (1945 dollars). She was sponsored by Mrs. Hilda Murrell whose son, Corporal Edward Earl Gyatt, USMC, was posthumously awarded the Purple Heart, Asian Pacific Campaign Medal and the Silver Star Medal for conspicuous gallantry in combat on the island of Tulagi in the Solomon Island chain.

In 1957, having had Terrier missiles and the first hydraulic stabilizer fins installed, *Gyatt* was designated DDG1, the world's first guided missile destroyer. *Gyatt* paved the way for the first generation of guided missile destroyers and cruisers in the Cold War Navy. In 1963, her missiles removed, *Gyatt* was redesignated DD 712 and, although assigned to Destroyer Squadron TWO, operated as a test platform for the Operational Test and Evaluation

Cdr. Louis Junod   **Cdr. Ed Elliott (in dark glasses)**

Force (OPTEVFOR) in Norfolk. From time to time, new designs were placed aboard for at-sea testing before being accepted for fleet use.

I RELIEVED LCDR Carl Solterer, a fine gentleman who was ordered to San Juan as executive officer of the naval facility there. (Coincidentally, we were to visit him in the not-too-distant future.) Our skipper was Cdr. Louis Junod, who had postgraduate credentials in ordnance. *Gyatt* was essentially excused from normal inter- and intra-squadron competition, coming under the operational control of the COMOPTEVFOR. Translation: *Gyatt* didn't shoot her guns, didn't exercise with submarines, didn't deploy to the Mediterranean, didn't do much more than mount new equipment and test it out. I had asked my detailer in the Bureau of Naval Personnel to please order me to a ship that was not deploying immediately, after my having been away for a year, but I didn't expect to end up on a ship that basically operated out of the normal fleet cycle. My disappointment was greater when, as Executive Officer, I sat down to study the personnel folders of my senior petty officers. I found that there were a lot of hardship cases, men who for one reason or another needed to be at sea – but not too much. They seemed to rotate from Norfolk home-

Me and Dad in *Gyatt*

Dad with Cdr. Elliott and his son, John Elliott

ported tenders (repair ships), to training centers to *Gyatt*. I had my mission. I was going to remind my petty officers what a real operating destroyer was like. I was going to turn *Gyatt* into a first-class destroyer.

THERE WASN'T MUCH we could do while in the shipyard, although we sent as many men to various fleet schools as possible. Sadly, I was mainly occupied with housekeeping chores, trying to motivate a fairly dispirited crew to take an interest in making the ship look sharp. My main help resided in the enthusiasm of Lt. William F. H. Glover III, a tall, imposing-looking South Carolinian, a graduate of the Naval Academy. Bill Glover had no patience with senior petty officers who spent their days drinking

**Lt. W. F. H. (Bill) Glover III
(Shown here as a Navy
Captain)**

coffee and watching the clock until time for liberty call. Together, we got the message across: Shape up or we will have you transferred to ships in the Far East or retired early. Certainly, without their cooperation, any promotion for them would be unrealized. They finally got the message. Upon leaving the shipyard we had a couple of weeks of independent ship exercise (ISE) in the Virginia Capes area – out on Monday, in on Friday. Bill and I hounded the Flotilla schedulers for air tracking and AA firing services and submarine training time for our ASW team. Our mantra was, if we had a piece of equipment, it must be made to work, and we must learn to use it properly. *Gyatt* was to leave shortly for refresher training under the rigorous Fleet Training Group (FTG) at Guantánamo Bay (GTMO), Cuba.

OUR VIRGINIA CAPES training complete, we operated with units of the U.S. Second Fleet before heading off to GTMO. From experience I knew that each ship arriving there had to have achieved a basic level of training in order to benefit from the (FTG) ship riders and services in Cuba. Realistically, this was seldom the case. But *Gyatt* was ready! Shortly after our arrival in GTMO, Commander E. C. Elliott relieved Cdr. Junod. The change-of-command ceremony was on the former missile deck; the weather was so hot that the blacktop decking melted on our white shoes. The new skipper called me to his cabin as soon as the old skipper had departed. "Hal," he said, "I know you have had a lot of destroyer experience, and I have previously commanded a destroyer escort. Here's how it's going to work: I command the ship, and you run it."

The very next morning I was able to test the seriousness of his statement. The word was passed, "Now go to your stations all the special sea and anchor detail." Getting underway called for our more experienced helmsman, lookouts, engineering personnel, signalmen and deck force to man their stations. The officer of the deck (OOD) was one of the more senior watch officers. I customarily gave the watch standers about ten minutes to get in place before going to the bridge. When I got there, I found Captain Elliott pacing around, smoking nervously. Saluting smartly I said, "Good morning, Captain; how are you this morning?"

"Fine," he growled, but I could see he was not enjoying the apparent confusion as every man found his place, checked out the various sound-powered phone circuits, and got the ship ready to get underway. Reports had to come to the bridge from the anchor detail on the forecastle, from the forward engine room, after-steering, etc. Getting up my courage, I approached the skipper. "Captain Elliott, I would appreciate your returning to your cabin. I will notify you when the ship is ready to get underway and then invite you to the bridge." Basically I was telling him to get out of the way. He reddened slightly, but caught on immediately. We exchanged light salutes; he turned and went below. This was to be the beginning of a great relationship, indeed, a friendship that lasted for many years until he passed away.

Refresher training was a boon to the crew. They worked energetically, operating all day and doing maintenance and correcting the day's training errors at night. It wasn't all work and no play. The official deck log reports the unofficial cargo on the O-1 deck aft, consisting of the XO's thirteen-foot runabout, maintained and used by the crew for recreation. Bill Glover and I took it out one Sunday. The engine died at the foot of McCalla

Field, the fixed-wing aviation landing terminal and runway. Bill started to climb up the hill when I reminded him that there were minefields in place since 1963. He scampered back and we paddled in.

But – miracle of miracles – *Gyatt* passed its Operational Readiness Inspection (ORI) in all departments. As Bill Glover still likes to say, "Yeah, I was gun boss and acting XO and you were Deputy CO."

We headed home on the winds of success, making liberty ports in San Juan, Puerto Rico and St. Thomas, Virgin Islands. Annabel and some of the other wives joined us and we were feted at the home of CDR Solterer and his wife, Honey.

MRS. HILDA MURRELL passed away in the summer of 1966, and her daughter wished the ship to have Corporal Gyatt's medals.

Receiving Corporal Gyatt's medals and citations from his sister in Syracuse, NY

So Annabel and I drove to Syracuse, New York, visited friends and places of interest along the way, and accepted the medals and citations on behalf of the USS *Gyatt*. It was the first time I had visited the university since I graduated in 1950. I could hardly recognize the old haunts; so much had changed on campus in fifteen years.

There were lots of other memorable occasions in *Gyatt*. We hosted a group of Navy Leaguers, one of whom was a state senator in Nebraska. He conferred on me the title of "Admiral of the Nebraska Navy." (Because Nebraska is a landlocked state, that honor placed me just a notch below a "Kentucky Colonel.") We were the "Gasparilla ship" for that Mardi Gras-like festival in Tampa, Florida. Our young sailors made a powerful impression on the women of Tampa. We went from Tampa to Miami and found many of the ladies waiting for our sailors on the pier upon our arrival. I hosted my Mom, Dad, and all their friends and relatives in South Florida for a barbecue on the fantail.

WE ENTERED THE SHIPYARD in Camden, New Jersey to have the first satellite navigation equipment in the world installed for evaluation. This got *Gyatt* a weekend in New York City, where I hosted Annabel's family and all of our friends for another barbecue on the fantail. We visited St. John, Canada, with its twenty-seven-foot tides and fantastic Bay of Fundy lobsters, and Boston where Ed and I went to a baseball game at Fenway Park and enjoyed one of the twilight performances of Hall of Famer Carl Yastrzemski. And finally, we used our satellite navigation equipment to precision-anchor the ship off the coast of Vieques, Puerto Rico, following which a major fleet amphibious exercise took place using *Gyatt* as the point of reference. Imagine, GPS in 1967.

One last mini-deployment chopped us to COMSUBLANT for duty as a missile range instrumentation ship, carrying a special telemetry hut and granting us the privilege of being on station less than half a mile from the submarine. With some trepidation, for we had seen films of runaway missiles barely missing escort destroyers, we were privileged to watch the first launch of the new Polaris A-3 ICBM. We greatly enjoyed a week's layover in Tenerife, one of the Canary Islands, followed by a stint as down-range missile instrumentation ship for another test-launch.

continued page 133

Onassis' *Christina*

E D ELLIOTT AND I had a sea-story adventure on our first day in St. Thomas. After conning the ship into port before first light we went to our cabins for a couple of hours of sleep. We woke up to find an enormous yacht anchored nearby. The bridge watch reported it to be *Christina*, Aristotle Onassis' mega-yacht, converted from a Canadian destroyer escort. "Get your dress whites on Hal, and have my gig lowered," Ed ordered, "We're going to pay a call on Mr. Onassis."

We spruced up and headed over to *Christina*, named after Onassis' daughter. At the top of the gangway we were greeted by a not-smiling officer who asked what we wanted. Advised that the U.S. Navy wished to welcome the yacht to our harbor and offer any assistance that might be needed, he softened, identified himself as the First Mate and asked if we would like a tour of the ship. Needless to say, we took him up on it and spent half an hour in awe of the luxurious conversion that had been done in Italy. In the forward saloon the furniture was Chippendale, anchored to the deck with tiny metal clips, paintings by Matisse and Picasso, and rare jade pieces the twins of which are owned by Queen Elizabeth. From there we viewed the two galleys, each with two chefs, two Greek and two French; the guest quarters, each named after a Greek island; and the two master staterooms. The first was Mr. Onassis's and had solid gold faucets in the sink and bathtub. The second was his mistress's, the world-renowned opera star, Maria Callas – with a circular bed that fit bulkhead-to-bulkhead in an alcove.

Topside, we were impressed by the collection of powerful launches and the amphibious aircraft operated by a retired Air France pilot. It would be lowered into the water by crane, and Mr. Onassis could travel for business or pleasure from any port. The radio shack contained the latest in single-sideband equipment.

We were escorted back to the gangway where, to our surprise and delight, Mr. Onassis himself came forward from the fantail in bathing suit and flip-flops. "Hey, Navy," he called, "Come back and have a drink."

So there we were – Ed Elliott, lace-curtain Irish from Boston, and Hal Sacks, Jewish kid from the Bronx – having drinks with Aristotle Onassis on his yacht. On the fantail (the aft end of the ship) was a mosaic-tiled swimming pool from which the water could be drained, and the floor raised to create a dance floor.

Mr. Onassis had a problem: He was going to San Juan next week and was unfamiliar with the berthing arrangements for such a large ship. Ed pointed to me and

The *Christina*, named for Aristotle Onassis's daughter

said, "Commander Sacks here is my navigator, and will be glad to show your captain how that port is set up. Do you have the charts?" In short order, a rather annoyed yacht captain appeared with the chart for San Juan harbor. I pointed out one navigation hazard and then showed him that the yacht basin was too small to accommodate a ship the size of *Christina*, and, of course, the commercial piers were usually occupied. I suggested the Navy Pier. Mr. Onassis commented that he had tied up there once before, "But that was when I had Churchill on board. Well, the Navy has always been good to me and perhaps they will let me tie up there."

All conversation ceased when Ms. Callas joined us. It was amazing to see the poised tycoon become immediately deferential to the great diva. Introductions were brief and, fortified with two large scotches on the rocks, I told Ms. Callas how thrilled I was to meet her and that I and some officers had once traveled from Naples to Milan to hear her perform at La Scala in *La Traviata*.

"Oh, you must be mistaken," she said. "I don't do that one any more."

"It was December of 1960," I replied.

"You know," she said, "that was the last time I performed that opera. You are very lucky!"

Other guests appeared including Countess X and her gigolo, and assorted nobility. It was time for us to leave, but just as we rose to go, we were asked if we had any movies on board. I promised to send a list of what we had and offered to deliver one, which we did. The "sea print" was returned by midnight, and when I awoke, *Christina* had slipped her moorings and headed out to sea. ★

Continued from page 129

SHORTLY AFTER RETURNING to Norfolk, I was awarded the Joint Services Commendation Medal for my tour in Vietnam. Promoted to Commander, I began thinking of my next tour of duty. I visited my detailer at the Bureau of Naval Personnel where we had a lively discussion. I insisted that I wanted a command, and command of a gunship which would deploy to Vietnam. "What makes you think you're qualified?" he asked. "You've only been a Commander for a few months." I had seen my fitness report from Ed. He recommended me for immediate command. I told the detailer that I had unusual qualifications, having done gunfire support in Korea, having taught gunfire support in GTMO, and having brought *Gyatt* through a satisfactory gunfire support qualifying shoot at Culebra.

Three weeks later I was ordered to walk across the pier from one ship in DESRON TWO to take command of USS *Steinaker* (DD863), in DESRON TWO, by reputation one of the top destroyers in the Atlantic Fleet. I would be the junior destroyer captain at the Naval Base in Norfolk, Virginia.

However, before I left *Gyatt* I attended to a few pieces of important business. Lt. (jg) Bob Williams (Willy) had done an outstanding job as ASW Officer and Navigator, as had Ensign Richard Greenamyer in the Weapons Department. So I arranged to have them ordered to Destroyer School in Newport, the school where I had worked on an Operations curriculum. Other skippers were short-sightedly reluctant to lose their best junior officers. But Captain Elliot supported my belief that we had an obligation to give a leg up to those with the greatest potential. In this case, it was a matter of "cast your bread upon the waters. . ."

CHAPTER TWELVE

★ ★ ★

Command at Sea

THE CHANGE OF COMMAND CEREMONY aboard a U.S. Navy ship is moving and simple. After a customary invocation, the departing Captain gets to make the speech. It is a time to review the vessel's achievements, thank the officers and crew, and their families, for the many sacrifices made, especially during extended deployments. The Captain then reads his orders. The relieving Captain makes no speech: he hasn't done anything yet. He reads his orders, salutes his predecessor, and says, "I relieve you, sir." The departing skipper's commission pennant is hauled down and a new pennant hoisted. There is usually a closing benediction.

So it was the morning of August 8, 1967. Our parents and kids were there along with some close friends. My mother at last could overcome her disappointment at not being able to speak of "My Son, the Doctor." Now she could speak of "My Son, the Captain!" The Catholic Chaplain gave the opening invocation; however, at my request Rabbi Arthur Steinberg, the Jewish Chaplain, gave the closing benediction, an uncommon occurrence on Navy ships. (Flash forward more than four decades and Rabbi Steinberg, now Rabbi Emeritus of Temple Sinai, Portsmouth, gave the invocation at the dedication of the Jewish War Veterans' Monument at the Jewish Community

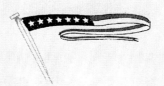

The Commanding Officer of the
United States Ship Steinaker
requests the pleasure of your company
at the Change of Command Ceremony
when Captain J. J. Tice III, U.S. Navy
will be relieved by
Commander H.H. Sacks, U.S.Navy
to be held on board
at Ten o'clock on Tuesday, the Eighth of August, 1967
United States Naval Base, Norfolk, Virginia

R.S.V.P.   Uniform: Service Dress White

Campus in Virginia Beach, in the construction of which I played a role).

USS *STEINAKER* (DD 863) was a World War II *Gearing*-class destroyer, commissioned near the end of the war on 26 May 1945. *Steinaker* deployed principally to the Mediterranean Sea with the Sixth Fleet until 1952, when she underwent conversion to a radar picket destroyer and was designated DDR 863. Her service continued to be primarily with the Atlantic Second and Mediterranean Sixth Fleets until 1963, including participation in the blockade of Cuba in 1962.

In 1964 *Steinaker* entered the shipyard to receive a major modernization under the Fleet Rehabilitation and Maintenance Program (FRAM), which equipped her for a significant antisubmarine warfare role. With an updated sonar suit, drone antisubmarine helicopters (DASH) capable of delivering homing antisubmarine torpedoes, and nuclear-tipped anti-submarine rockets (ASROC), she served once again in the Mediterranean and Mideast Forces.

Now *Steinaker* proceeded in her antisubmarine warfare (ASW) mission with a specific objective – preparing for the first combat deployment of her career seven months hence. *Steinaker* was scheduled to sail in March of 1968 for duty with the Seventh Fleet in the South China Sea and the Gulf of Tonkin. Her new Captain was faced with the task of replacing the imprint of the previous commanding officer with his own, both on the officers in the wardroom, and in the mess decks, on the crew.

During a successful at-sea period, conducting ASW exercises, some items of concern surfaced. For example, our DASH helicopters were used extensively and I soon learned that they were seldom flown as there was always a chance that one would be lost (shades of our lost torpedoes aboard USS *Owen*!). That would be a black mark against the command. My view was that failure to fly them would discourage the maintenance personnel, making a loss more likely.

We returned to port to welcome aboard Lt. (Lcdr-selectee) Leslie Palmer, who relieved Cdr Hughes as XO. Someone in the Bureau of Personnel must have had a good laugh, assigning the most junior Executive Officer in the Norfolk destroyer force to the most junior Captain. I confess this added to my concerns. This young officer had served in a destroyer escort and a minesweeper. As the principal training officer aboard, was he up to the task of preparing *Steinaker* for an extended deployment in a combat zone? Having learned that we had not fired the guns in recent memory and that we hadn't exercised at handling our nuclear weapons, I was greatly aware of the training regimen ahead of us.

Almost immediately after Lt. Palmer reported aboard,

we were told to prepare for an NTPI, a complex inspection of our handling of our nuclear-tipped ASROC missiles and our administration of the system records. Palmer and our Weapons Officer, Lt. Hugh Carroll, had become friends and neighbors. They worked tirelessly to bring us up to speed – to no avail. We failed miserably. Within three months we would have to pass a re-test or face the embarrassment of having our ASROC missiles removed.

OUR NEXT CHALLENGE was to qualify at gunfire support. If not qualified *Steinaker* would not be permitted to serve on the gun line off Vietnam, and would be limited to rescue destroyer duty behind the aircraft carriers. My whole motivation for obtaining this command would be shattered. This time I pitched in to assist in the preparation for our live shooting exercise at Bloodsworth Island in Chesapeake Bay, at the southern end of Dorchester County, Maryland. The live fire exercise was an all day affair in which the ship was required to demonstrate its ability to respond to a "call for fire" from the Shore Fire Control Party (SFCP), plot the target while underway, lay the guns on target, fire initial rounds at the command of the SFCP, adjust the fire as directed by the spotters, and fire for effect. An important exercise measured the ability of the ship to spot counter battery fire from enemy gun emplacements while conducting a fire mission, shift fire to defend the ship, and then complete the mission. The "graduation exercise" included the firing of illumination shells to assist the spotter in locating the target, and then completing the fire mission while maintaining continuous illumination.

The long trip up the Chesapeake required the navigation team to be up throughout the night until morning revealed Bloodsworth Island, a long, low sandbar wrapped in haze. By the time the SFCP arrived and set up for the exercise, the sun was high and the day was hot and humid. Nothing seemed to go right.

The first run through was an outright disaster. The second and third were little better. By late afternoon the crew was frustrated with defeat. With the sun lowering on the horizon I called the SFCP on our tactical radio and asked them if we could take a one-hour break, then come back and try one last time. They agreed to remain on the range past the regular stopping time, but not past 9 PM.

I secured the crew from General Quarters (GQ) and called the XO and Weapons Officer to the bridge. "Les, feed the men and let them get a quick shower. Hugh, take a breather and then get your petty officers together and go over our mistakes. We will go to GQ in one hour and give it our best." They had come to the bridge expecting to hear that I had given up. The relief on their faces was palpable. An hour later, we returned to firing stations and raced through the shoots, barely able in the dimming light to see the smoke pot signifying counter-battery. Our illumination firing was for real, as darkness had closed in when we completed what would be scored as a perfect exercise. *Steinaker* had qualified in Gunfire Support. More importantly our young XO had an epiphany: With a little help from his skipper, he had made it happen and he never looked back in defeat again.

We headed down the Bay to the Destroyer-Submarine Piers in a jubilant mood.

Hugh Carroll reminded me that he had an important sonar calibration to perform the next morning that would require us mooring bow out. We approached harbor shortly after midnight and requested permission to enter port, advising Port Control we would be mooring stern first and that the assistance of a tug or pusher boat would be appreciated.

"Steinaker," came the reply, "we regret no assistance is available at this hour therefore we can assign you to an anchorage for the night and move you alongside in the morning."

I elected to moor without assistance and was assigned

a berth "starboard side to" alongside the three ships in our division. I called to the bridge Ensign Bob Patton, a young Naval Academy graduate who was in charge of the foc's'l at sea detail. "Mr. Patton," I ordered, "make the port anchor ready for letting go, and when I say 'let go,' drop the port anchor underfoot at the short stay." "Aye! Aye! Captain." Patton saluted and raced off.

Landings in the Elizabeth River were affected by three factors: wind, current, and tide. Sometimes they exerted a combined force. Sometimes they worked against each other. On that early morning, the wind and current would be setting me down onto the pier. However, since I was landing not alongside the pier itself but alongside a sister ship, extra caution was called for. I turned the ship around and began backing down rather swiftly to enable me to get parallel to the other ship before wind and current took hold. Just when it looked like I would slam into the outboard destroyer I shouted, "LET GO!" Down splashed the 4,000 pound anchor, braking our progress. "ALL ENGINES STOP. RUDDER AMIDSHIPS." And the *Steinaker* just nestled alongside. The astonished and only half-awake line-handlers on the outboard ship received all lines smartly and I hustled ashore to call Annabel to please come pick up a very tired but very happy skipper.

In the morning I learned that the Flotilla duty officer notified the Admiral that some crazy skipper was attempting a stern-to landing at night without any assistance. Little did I know that many senior eyes were upon us. Shortly, a messenger arrived with a note from the Admiral:

> *Dear Captain Sacks: Those of us who watched your*
> *stern-to landing last night learned what can be done with a*
> *destroyer with skill, courage, and a little bit of luck.*
> *Well done!*

I knew I was an excellent ship handler. More importantly,

now the crew knew, as a copy of the Admiral's note was placed on the crew's bulletin board by the XO. For some reason, destroyermen love to either brag about or bemoan their skipper's skill or lack of skill driving the ship. Morale was definitely improving. We had passed one crucial test and now had to prepare for the retake of our NTPI. The Navy had plans for *Steinaker* that would give us the perfect training opportunity.

IMPROVED MORALE WAS of particular importance at this time as *Steinaker* faced the loss of 89 seamen and petty officers whose tours of duty would end in the middle of our deployment to Vietnam. They would be replaced mostly with inexperienced first tour sailors. I called a meeting of these men in the mess decks and told them that *Steinaker* would make it to the western Pacific and back with or without them, but that to achieve excellence *Steinaker* needed their experience. I also challenged them to be part of this defining moment in history. Seventy-nine voluntarily extended their tours or their enlistments to complete this cruise.

USS *Steinaker*, in 1967 the Navy's most sophisticated ASW destroyer, was assigned to the Atlantic Fleet Submarine Force for extended operations as a missile range instrumentation ship in support of the first test launching of the newest intercontinental ballistic missile (ICBM), the Poseidon. Once again, experience paid off. While serving as XO of *Gyatt* we were "chopped" to SUBLANT to serve as missile range instrumentation ship for a test launch of the Polaris A-1 missile. I clearly recall the period as being one of long stretches of utter boredom, steaming slowly to the launch site in the mid-Atlantic. This was followed by a few minutes of great tension, circling the launching submarine at a distance of only a half-mile, knowing that test missiles had on occasion flipped over and narrowly missed striking the escorting destroyer. But boring steaming was just what the doctor ordered for *Steinaker*, as the crew had days upon days to train, train, and train some more. The much-dreaded NTPI was awaiting our return to Norfolk.

BUT IT WASN'T ALL TRAINING. Between missile shoots, we had five days in Las Palmas. Les Palmer, Hugh Carroll and I became expert samplers of the local Sangria while sunning and swimming at the strange beaches of black volcanic sand. And on the way home, *Steinaker* made a one-day fuel stop in Bermuda where the crew enjoyed a Navy-style softball game, with a case of cold beer at every base. *Steinaker* received a "Well Done" in a commendatory letter from Vice Admiral Schade, Commander of the Atlantic Fleet Submarine Force. But the Admiral's "Well Done" paled in intensity when measured with the "not so well done" received from the mail-starved distaff side of the command:

THE: GOOD SHIP LOLLIPOP

(Our motto: They also serve who only stand and wait ... and wait and wait.....)

Cdr. H. H Sacks, Commanding Officer USS STEINAKER (DD863) c/o Fleet Post Office, New York, NY 09501

Dear Cdr. Sacks:

We are indeed happy to hear that the STEINAKER is continuing its mission of keeping peace while spreading good will for the American people in Port Canaveral, Fort Lauderdale (where two days passed much too rapidly), St. Thomas (after three arduous days at sea, the mountains of St. Thomas rising above the horizon seemed a veritable paradise), San Juan (providing a completely different pace and atmosphere least anyone be bored by the same old paradises), and

Las Palmas (for ten days of much-needed rest and rehabilitation after a grueling two weeks at sea).

We are indeed convinced that everything possible is being done to make the men of STEINAKER the most satisfied men in the Navy. As for the wives – they seem to be stacking up as the least satisfied wives in the Navy; no color television, no popcorn machine, and no baseball cap with the big "863" in front.

Home life continues to be arduous but we are continuing to seek opportunities to add relaxation and entertainment to our daily work schedule. Norfolk is a city of great variety – A&Ps, Colonial Stores, Food Fairs, and Giants abound – if you get bored with the Commissary. If time hangs heavy, there are numerous car washes to run through. Several exciting get-togethers have taken place at such veritable paradises as Poplar Halls and Crown Point. Current plans include a safari to Kings in the neighboring city of Virginia Beach.

The children are collectively well. Current tabulations indicate eight noses running, five kids a-coughing, two 24-hour viruses, and a bandage on a bare knee. Money is generally scarce and plans are in the works tor a benefit cake sale to supplement meager receipts.

If for any reason you wish to get in touch with the wives, put a note in a bottle – it's as quick as the mail service. It is Our policy to keep the men of STEINAKER informed of what their families are doing, where they are going, and what their names are. Every few months you can expect to receive another Gamily-Fram – in fact, every few years should be enough as nothing much happens every few months.

It is our desire to maintain a constant and strong link between the Wives and men who serve aboard STEINAKER; however the Navy does everything in its power to make this impossible. If you encounter any questions or problems which you feel necessitate attention or assistance, please feel free to write to Dear Abby – she has all the answers.

Sincerely
A. Sacks, Wife (I think) of Commanding Officer

An important lesson was learned here and during our deployments to Vietnam. We made certain to maintain better lines of communication with our dependents.

WE PUT IN TO CAPE CANAVERAL to drop off the telemetry hut and left immediately to begin our pre-deployment tender availability, a three-week opportunity to ready the ship in every way possible for the eight month deployment ahead. Heading back to Norfolk, *Steinaker* encountered very heavy seas on the bow. Anxious to get home I struggled to make the best speed possible. However, a freak wave, of greater strength than what we had been experiencing damaged the shield and the roller path of our forward twin 5"38 caliber gun mount, half of our shore bombardment battery. I was despondent, knowing that at this level of repair was beyond the capacity of the tender and putting *Steinaker* into the shipyard might postpone or even cancel our deployment. My "cumshaw"[1] specialists found a complete gun mount in storage at the shipyard and, with a little arm twisting,

---

[1]"cumshaw" is a slang term, possibly from the old China Service fleet of pre-WWII vintage. I couldn't find it in the *Dictionary of Navy Slang*, but it refers to an informal system of barter, bypassing any normal procurement system.

JOHNNY CARSON REMEMBERED

USS *STEINAKER* (DD 863) made a port call in Fort Lauderdale, Florida in 1968, shortly before commencing its pre-deployment tender availability in Norfolk. My XO, the late Lcdr. Les Palmer, and I went ashore to visit a well-known tourist attraction, a Polynesian restaurant known as the "Maikai." Seated at the bar, I glanced over my shoulder and noted Johnny Carson and Ed McMahon enjoying a drink in a nearby booth. Knowing Johnny and Ed to have served in the Navy and Marines, respectively, I sent my card with compliments to them. They immediately asked us to join them and we spent an enjoyable evening swapping sea stories (Johnny really had warm memories of his service and asked serious questions about the "new" Navy) while we dined. We stayed to watch the floor show, which, it turned out, was the reason Carson was there. He wanted to show support for a somewhat down-and-out comedian he knew from the "old" days.

I invited Johnny and Ed to visit the ship, assuming he would politely decline. But no, he said, "Let's go!" and so at 0200 hours, the four of us greeted a surprised OOD and headed for the wardroom. Johnny said he was hungry and Les offered to wake the duty steward.

I intervened, went into wardroom galley with Ed and together we rustled up coffee, scrambled eggs and toast.

More Navy talk ensued until about 0400 when I offered to drive them to their hotel. Johnny wouldn't have it but insisted on calling a taxi. We piped him off at 0430. ★

Lt. Carroll convinced the tender that it could simply lift the old mount off and lower the new mount into position. It was a huge task, and the repair ship's people worked long hours alongside my gunner's mates to complete the task.

I was immensely relieved when *Steinaker* passed its NTPI with an alomst-perfect score. Now we were free to grant some leave, particularly to sailors with families, in order to do whatever was necessary before departing.

ON 30 MARCH, 1968, along with our sister ships in Destroyer Division 21, USS *Blandy* (DD943), USS *Borie* (DD 704), and USS *Rich* (DD 820), *Steinaker* departed Norfolk on its Westpac tour of duty. Captain Frank C. Dunham, Commander Destroyer Squadron 2 and Commander Destroyer Division 21 was embarked in *Blandy*.

There is no question but that this tour was the highlight of my life at this point in my career and was doubtless a defining moment in the coming of age of my young crew.

Lest this chapter be a book unto itself, I am attaching as an Appendix the text of a previously published pamphlet, *Excerpts from the Captain's Log*. Re-reading these contemporary reports from the vantage point of four decades, I realize there are many changes I might wish to make. They speak for themselves; however, so I will leave them as is.

In the next chapter I will take the liberty of highlighting a few memorable incidents while wrapping up the best tour of my career.

THE FOLLOWING PHOTOS highlight my outstanding Executive Officer, Les Palmer, and our department heads who were responsible for making *Steinaker* a pleasure to command.

Lieutenant Commander Leslie N. Palmer, U.S. Navy

Lieutenant Commander Leslie N. Palmer, USN, a native of Baltimore, Maryland, was graduated from Baltimore Polytechnic Institute in 1955 and that summer entered the U.S. Naval Academy, Annapolis, Maryland. He graduated and was commissioned Ensign on June 3, 1959.

Following graduation from the Naval Academy, he was assigned to the destroyer escort USS CLAUD JONES, where he served initially as Combat Information Center Officer and later as Operations Officer. In July 1962, he was transferred to the ocean minesweeper USS DASH where he completed a tour as Executive Officer in 1964.

After a three year tour at the Bureau of Naval Personnel in Washington, D.C., Lieutenant Commander Palmer was ordered to duty as Executive Officer of the USS STEINAKER.

Lieutenant Commander Palmer is married to the former Miss JoAnn V. Quinn of Baltimore, Maryland. They have a daughter, Jodi, age 8 and a son, Michael, age 5.

Left side, top to bottom: **Riding a LARC into Phan Tiet; Pointing to gun flashes from North Vietnamese shore battery; Drawing sidearms.**

LT H.E. Carroll
WEAPONS OFFICER

LT R.R. Williams
OPERATIONS OFFICER

DEPARTMENT HEADS

LT R.M. Esposito
CHIEF ENGINEER

LTJG C.J. Horsch
SUPPLY OFFICER

Steinaker department heads under my command

Presenting the "last round fired in combat" to Commodore Dunham

Mom and me

At the Conn

The seal of *Steinaker*

Commodore Dunham pinning Bronze Star Medal with
Combat "V"

UNITED STATES SEVENTH FLEET

The President of the United States takes pleasure in presenting

the Bronze Star Medal to

Commander Harold H. SACKS
United States Navy

for service as set forth in the following:

<u>CITATION</u>

"For meritorious service while serving as Commanding Officer of USS STEINAKER (DD-863) from 13 May to 1 October 1968 during combat operations against the enemy. Commander SACKS displayed exceptional qualities of leadership while directing his ship in the execution of a wide variety of tasks, including Operation Sea Dragon, naval gunfire support, carrier escort and picket duties. His personal example inspired his officers and men to maximum performance and the highest degree of combat readiness. His efforts to enhance working relationships and understanding with Vietnamese allies ashore contributed to the effectiveness of naval gunfire support in the area. On one occasion, STEINAKER was taken under intense and accurate fire by enemy shore batteries. By his skill and alert judgment, he maneuvered his ship to escape unscathed and to bring effective counter-battery fire to bear. Through his professional competence, STEINAKER inflicted significant damage upon the enemy's personnel and material resources. Commander SACKS' leadership, professionalism, and loyal devotion to duty reflected great credit upon himself and were in keeping with the highest traditions of the United States Naval Service."

Commander SACKS is authorized to wear the Combat "V".

For the President

W. F. BRINGLE
Vice Admiral
United States Navy

Bronze Star Citation

CHAPTER THIRTEEN

★ ★ ★

Wrapping Up the Command Tour

S*TEINAKER* AND THE SQUADRON anchored off Little Creek the night before our official arrival at the Norfolk Naval Base in order to "titivate" the ship after our long journey home. What was one more day to wait for family reunions after eight months of separation?

Commodore Dunham was preparing a coordinated logistics requirement (LOGREQ) message and asked each skipper what was needed upon arrival in addition to fuel, water, electric power and telephone service. He added that he would order a tug and pilot to assist each ship in berthing. I immediately requested "NO TUG AND PILOT FOR STEINAKER," figuring that this was probably the last time I would bring her alongside and, with family and friends watching, nothing would deter me from making my own landing. As it turned out the squadron got underway from anchorage and steamed into the Destroyer Piers into the teeth of a fresh breeze. Despite wind and current, *Steinaker*'s approach was perfect and all lines were over briskly. We were home at last!

Steinaker would soon enter the Norfolk Naval Shipyard in Portsmouth, Virginia for a major overhaul, having been an unprecedented forty-eight months out of drydock. But there were moments of the Westpac cruise to savor and major changes in personnel to deal with.

Some of the moments that will be recalled whenever two or more members of our crew get together include the following:

MOST MEMORABLY, it turned out that Passover would occur while *Steinaker* was in transit from San Diego to Pearl Harbor. I had prearranged with the Chaplaincy Commission of the Jewish Welfare Board (now the Jewish Community Center Association) for Passover supplies to be shipped to San Diego. We loaded matzo, gefilte fish, matzo ball soup with chicken, *hagaddot*, *kepot*, and sacramental wine. With the permission and encouragement of my fellow DESRON TWO skippers and Commodore Frank Dunham, Jewish personnel from the other seven ships in the squadron were transferred to *Steinaker* for the transit, and a wonderful Seder meal and ceremony were held in our wardroom.

ONE OF THE PROBLEMS afflicting the Drone Anti-submarine Helicopter (DASH) program was the inordinate fear commanding officers had of losing a "bird." (I'm guessing that in 1968 dollars they cost about $200,000.) This fear prompted skippers to simply not fly the DASH more than the required minimum few hours every three months. The result was that the DASH crews had little motivation to perform required maintenance on a system so seldom used. Thus the likelihood of a casualty increased. I, however, was fascinated by the system. Now, almost half a century later, advanced technology has made the use of drone surveillance and weapons delivery systems common and the future of some categories of manned aircraft doubtful. But this was 1968, and the airborne control of the DASH clung to a slim radio transmission from the controller on the ship. Before sailing, I visited the other ships in our division and spoke to their DASH officers. I encouraged them to exchange radio frequencies so that in an emergency they could assume control of each others' DASH.

When *Steinaker* left the Panama Canal for San Diego, California, we decided to try to set a new fleet record by keeping one DASH continuously airborne for six days and nights. This was to be accomplished by putting a DASH requiring recovery for refueling into an automatic hover, then launching our second DASH, putting it into automatic hover and then recovering and refueling the first one. This went on day and night, the maintenance crews working 12-hour shifts and Ltjg Chuck Spencer doing most of the controlling with brief relief from his leading technician and Lt. (jg) Denny Connor. On the sixth day, having set a new fleet record, *Steinaker* suffered an engineering casualty, losing all electrical power. The airborne DASH, receiving no signal from the ship, went into an automatic hover. Spencer advised me that it had about 45 minutes of fuel remaining. Using visual signals, since we had no power, we were able to get the USS *Borie* to close us. Again, using hand signals, we advised them of the situation and requested that their DASH officer set up our control frequency. After about 25 minutes of tense waiting we

Lt. (jg) Chuck Spencer – DASH Officer

USS *Borie* with three DASH units, their two (*top*) and one of *Steinaker*'s

were elated to see *Borie* take control of our DASH and land it on her flight deck. Needless to say, we had to buy a lot of drinks for the *Borie* DASH team on arrival in San Diego. (Subsequently in Westpac, although strictly forbidden, we used our DASH to transfer needed spare parts to our sister ships.)

STEINAKER WAS ON PICKET DUTY off the DMZ (the demilitarized zone just north of Quang Tri Province, separating North and South Vietnam) conducting a random patrol. *Blandy*, our squadron flagship, was in an adjacent sector conducting her patrol. It was shortly after 2200 on a particularly black night. Off-duty officers on both ships, including both skippers and Commodore Frank Dunham, were in their respective wardrooms watching movies. From the signal bridge came a sound-powered telephone call:

"Captain, we are being challenged by the *Blandy*!"

"Well, give them the response!"

"But Captain, they are using the wrong challenge. They are using the small boat challenge."

"Then ignore it and send the following from CO to Commodore: 'Only a friend passing in the night'."

"Captain, the following crossed with your message: 'The first challenge was a warning. The second could be dangerous – signed: Commodore.'"

"Send the following to the Commodore: *'Cancel my last.'*"

STEINAKER WAS PROCEEDING to Subic Bay in the Philippines from Danang, Vietnam, where we had returned a photo-reconnaissance drone that we retrieved following its crash. Annabel and several of the wives were on their way to Subic Bay to meet the ship and I was understandably in a hurry to get there. I plotted a course that would save several hours by crossing to the landward side of Tiger Island. I was in the wardroom having lunch. Our Supply Officer, Lt. (jg) Chris Horsch, having studied and qualified as Officer of the Deck Underway (Independent Steaming), had the conn. Suddenly the General Alarm sounded, and the 1MC announced, "All hands man your battle stations! This is not a drill! Counter battery! Counter battery! All hands man your battle stations!

I bolted to the bridge to see heavy mortar splashes to starboard and relieved our much relieved Supply Officer of the conn. My XO, LCDR Les Palmer went to the Combat

Information Center and Weapons Officer, Lt. Hugh Carroll, headed for the main battery director. We commenced maneuver-ing to open the range from the island, but in small increments so as not to lose speed. On occasion, when it seemed they had us straddled, I turned toward the island to throw their laddering off. Lt. Carroll opened fire with our after mount and a spotter plane in the vicinity helped to coach him on target. We scored some good hits, took none ourselves, and cleared the area. Suddenly, a voice came over the primary tactical circuit, "Hal Sacks! Is that you out there?"

I recognized the voice of Commodore John Smith, the Gun Line Commander and an old friend who was flagship Captain of USS *Davis* when I was a lieutenant serving as DESRON 12 Operations Officer. "Good afternoon, Commodore," I replied.

"Hal, what the hell are you doing there?" he asked. I lamely offered that I was taking a shortcut to meet Annabel in Subic Bay.

He laughed and replied, "Good thing you didn't get hit. Anyway, good shooting and give her a hug for me. Out!"

ENROUTE TO YOKOSUKA for much-needed R & R, the ship had to transit the Shimonoseki Straits at night. Ensign Bob Patton, newly qualified as Officer of the Deck (Underway), had the deck and the conn when we were surrounded by tiny Japanese fishing boats, miles out to sea, determined to come as close to us as possible. Patton was swallowing hard and looked to me for guidance in dealing with literally dozens of closing contacts. I leaned over and repeated the exact words I had heard from my skipper fifteen years before: "Steer your course. Don't worry about the fishing boats. They will be watching you and will avoid you. But if by chance you hit one, for God's sake, don't stop – just keep going." Ensign Patton completed his watch and, more than four decades later, retired Navy Captain Patton can repeat those words verbatim.

ENROUTE TO YOKOSUKA I received a telegram from Tony Shimazu, proprietor of the Sun Laundry and Dry Cleaning Company (*see Chapter 2*). "Dear Captain Sacks, I see that your ship will be arriving in Yokosuka shortly." (How he knew of our classified movements was a question still unanswered.) "Captain," he continued, "Perhaps you will remember me. I am the man who brought your dry-cleaned uniform to you fifteen years ago, and I will be waiting on the pier when your ship arrives to welcome you." Sure enough, there on the pier was Tony, now grey-haired and a bit stockier. He was carrying a huge bundle of flowers. We embraced on the quarterdeck and he came up to the wardroom where he promptly invited me and some of the officers to a special dinner that evening. We all enjoyed a traditional meal of sushi and sukiyaki with copious bottles of sake. What a remarkable tribute!

STEINAKER BRIEFLY JOINED an operation called "Market Time" which was set up to intercept and destroy the maritime shipment of contraband from North to South by sea. Under the Rules of Engagement established for such operations, legitimate fishing craft could be tracked on radar heading essentially East/West from the shore, and would thus not be bothered. Craft tracking North/South were by definition considered to be infiltrators and were fair game for our gunners. One of the problems we faced were that these light wooden boats, even when directly hit by our 5" high capacity projectiles, would suffer little more than an easily plugged five-inch hole; the impact was insufficient to set off the fuse that would detonate the round. The solution was found in our large inventory of WWII 5" proximity fused anti-aircraft ammunition. When fired at an aircraft, the electronic fuse caused detonation within about 50 feet of the target. If the round did not come close enough to explode, it would detonate at about 50 feet above the ocean on its descent. *Steinaker* fired these rounds at North/South infiltrating boats and in one day of shooting, with the assistance of an airborne spotter, shattered over 30 boats.

FINALLY, A BRIEF NOTE about how the "Old Man" celebrated his 38th birthday. August 2, 1968. the ship was at anchor off Phan Thiet in the III Corp area of South Vietnam. Leaving the XO in charge, I had my gig launched and took it ashore. I had arranged for a jeep to take me to the rough airstrip operated jointly by U.S. and ARVN forces. A U.S. Air Force forward air controller (FAC) welcomed me aboard his single-engine spotter plane. Off we went flying low over the jungle. Checking in with the Marine gunnery liaison officer (GLO), we received a "call for fire" and relayed the target information to *Steinaker*. Imagine the surprise in CIC when they heard the target coordinates coming from their airborne Captain. *Steinaker* opened fire and I spotted their rounds on to the target (a VC supply cache) until I ordered them to "fire for effect." Despite having worked as a spotter in Korea, I was unprepared for the radical maneuvering of the spotter plane keeping the target in sight. It was all I could do to keep my stomach from betraying me. My appreciation and admiration for the FACs who did this three and four times a day, every day, greatly deepened.

ONE OF THE FIRST personnel changes was the departure of my outstanding Executive Officer, **LCDR Les Palmer.** Les had asked me for permission to apply for the job of Naval Aide to the Vice President of the United States. Of course, I granted permission and wrote a strong recommendation. Les got the job and departed *Steinaker* to serve as aide to the controversial Vice President, Spiro Agnew. Les went on from there to command a destroyer and ultimately was awarded flag rank and was ordered to the U.S. Naval Academy as Commandant of Midshipmen. Tragically, at age 47, Les was fatally stricken by a heart attack

THE SECRETARY OF THE NAVY
WASHINGTON

1 4 MAR 1969

Commander Harold H. Sacks, USN
Commanding Officer
U.S.S. STEINAKER (DD-863)
Fleet Post Office
New York, New York 09501

Dear Captain Sacks:

My visit to STEINAKER on Wednesday was certainly
most helpful and enjoyable. STEINAKER is the first
destroyer I have been aboard since becoming Secretary
of the Navy and I will think of this often as I deal
with destroyer questions in the future.

The explanations that you and your officers gave
me were both well planned and clear. They certainly
helped me fill some of the many gaps in my brief
education as Secretary.

I was particularly appreciative of your thought-
fulness in giving me the ashtray from the last 5-inch
round you fired in Vietnam, and it will be a memento
of a very pleasant visit on STEINAKER. I only wish
the visit could have been longer and there could have
been time for more leisurely discussions with you and
your officers.

I hope you will pass my appreciation to all those
who played a part in making my visit so successful.

With warm personal regards.

Sincerely yours,

JOHN H. CHAFEE

while jogging. Aboard *Steinaker*, he fulfilled the XO role with great distinction.

Lt. Hugh Carroll, our Weapons Officer, went on to post-graduate work leading to an MS, served as XO of USS *Blakely* (FF1072) and commanded a new guided missile frigate USS *Jack Williams* (FFG-21). After several major positions as a Captain in the Navy, Hugh concluded his Navy career as Commodore of the facility charged with training in the safe handling of tactical nuclear weapons for the Atlantic Fleet.

Lt. Robert (Bob) Williams ("Willy"), who had previously served in *Gyatt* with me, following postgraduate school, commanded USS *Canon* (PG-90), was XO/CO of USS *John S. McCain* (DDG 36), XO USS *Paul Foster* (DD 964), CO USS *Hewitt* (DD 966) and served as Commodore of Destroyer Squadron 5.

Lt. Rich Greenamyer, who had also previously served with me in *Gyatt*, following his tour as Engineering Officer aboard *Steinaker*, proceeded to post-graduate school and converted from Line Officer to Engineering Duty Only (EDO). He served as Project Officer for new ship construction under the Supervisor of Shipbuilding in Seattle; as Repair Officer aboard USS *Bryce Canyon* (AD 36), a destroyer tender; as Maintenance Officer for the Commander in Chief, U.S. Pacific Fleet; and as Planning and Estimating Officer at the Pearl Harbor Shipyard.

Ensign Bob Patton, destined to be the junior officer aboard *Steinaker* for the entire deployment, took on all the collateral duties dumped on him with professional seriousness and good humor. When Hugh Carroll left the ship, Bob fleeted up to Weapons Officer and subsequently served as Weapons Officer on another ship before being ordered as a LT as XO USS *Mitscher.* He was then early-selected to LCDR and after a tour as

Chief Staff Officer for a DESRON became CO of USS *John L. Hall* (FFG 32). Once again he relieved Hugh Carroll, this time as Operations Officer for the Commander of Naval Surface Forces, Atlantic (COMNAVSURFLANT). He commanded the USS *Leyte Gulf* (CG 55) as the crowning achievement of his shipboard career.

AN OBSERVANT READER will note the caption accompanying the photo of me presenting our Commodore with an ashtray (*page 148*) and here, to the Secretary of the Navy John Chafee. The ashtrays were fabricated from "the last round fired in combat." Just before our last fire mission, I asked Hugh Carroll

Presenting the "last round fired in combat" to Secretary of the Navy Chafee

how many rounds of actual brass powder we had (by this time brass was used only for 'short' charges).

"Twelve, sir," he replied. "Well, use them up on our last mission and have them made into souvenir ashtrays." Each was inscribed as the "last round fired in combat." I gave one to each of my department heads and to our XO, keeping one for myself. The others were given to such dignitaries as the Commodore, Adm. Jack Wadleigh, our flotilla commander, Secretary of the Navy John Chafee, and the Commander in Chief, U.S. Atlantic Fleet. Commodore Dunham quickly caught on as he was present at most of the presentations. He struggled to keep from laughing each time.

Captain Sacks discusses a piece of equipment with Secretary of the Navy
John Chafee, Admiral Ephraim Holmes, CINCLANTFLT, Commodore
Frank Dunham, and Captain Stansfield Turner (future director CIA)

STEINAKER UNDERWENT a very successful overhaul for
which we received a commendation from the fleet commander. I
was relieved by Commander Billy Earl. *Steinaker* unfortunately
grounded during NATO operations in Norwegian waters and
subsequently was transferred to the reserve fleet, serving to train
reservists in the Washington, DC area. She was transferred to
the Mexican navy and was renamed the ARM *Netzahualcoyotl* (D-
102). She served for decades and was still in service as late as
2013, at which time she and the USS *Henderson* (DD 785) (in the
Portuguese Navy) were the only two ships afloat armed with the
awesome 5"/38 caliber guns.

As my tour came to an end I naturally contacted my detailer
in the Bureau of Naval Personnel (BUPERS) and was told that I
was about to be ordered to the Naval War College in Newport,

Steinaker **in drydock, 1969.**
My last task was to get the ship
overhauled before being relieved.

RI. Having just completed five years of Vietnam and sea duty, the thought of uprooting my family for a nine-month tour was unappealing. I had already served on a joint staff and earned a graduate degree, and I didn't see the professional necessity for the War College, prestigious though it was. I requested duty in Norfolk, and was ordered to the staff of Commander Antisubmarine Warfare Forces U.S. Atlantic Fleet (COMASWFOR-LANT) as Assistant Chief of Staff, Intelligence. COMASWFORLANT was a three-star command with additional duty as COMOCEAN-SYSLANT (the Atlantic Sosus system – a submerged hydrophone system designed to help track Soviet submarines) and as COMOCEANSLANT (a parallel NATO command when operating jointly).

CHAPTER FOURTEEN

★ ★ ★

COMASWFORLANT

A S WE HAVE NOTED, change of command in the Navy is an emotional nevent for both the skipper being relieved and the skipper taking over. The skipper being relieved gets to make the speech, reviewing the highlights of his tour, thanking his family, his crew and their families, and anything else he wants to say. The skipper taking command hasn't done anything to talk about yet. He just reads his orders, salutes smartly and says, "I relieve you sir."

So I got to make my speech. The ship's commission pennant was hauled down and eventually given to me mounted and framed. We repaired to the Officers' Club for a reception and I gradually realized that it was over; the greatest professional experience of my life had come to a close. But the challenges were not.

Vice Admiral Paul Masterton, an aviator, was Commander U.S. Anti-Submarine Forces Atlantic (COMASWFORLANT) and had the reputation of disliking intelligence officers, all of whom he called "spooks." Fortunately, balancing this negative attitude, Captain Frank Dunham, my Commodore and friend in DESRON Two, was concurrently ordered as Chief of Staff. It was comforting to know that I had someone in my corner.

My office was in the ASW Commander's Operations Control Center (OPCON), located in the Fleet Commander's OPCON

Center. Behind secure doors my little empire consisted of five junior watch officer analysts, a LCDR Intelligence Specialist, and an administrative assistant. I shared our OPCON Center with

Vice Adm. Paul Masterton. Photo is inscribed "To Hal The world's greatest ASW "spook." All the best. Paul Masterton"

the Current Operations Officer, Captain Al Hibbs, an articulate, very Irish aviator whose experience was primarily in the patrol aircraft community. He had the reputation of chewing up commanders at breakfast and spitting them out at lunch.

Once again, experience gained in previous tours paid off. From the days of my tours at STIC and MACV, I had developed a specialty in frustrating the overprotective ploys of intelligence specialists. They tended to keep an overly-tight hold on intelligence vitally needed by the operating forces to accomplish their mission and, in some cases, merely to survive. Of course, there was also a need to protect sensitive sources. But I built my reputation on finding a way to get the information needed to the operating forces. In Vietnam my "RELIABLE AGENT" reports *(see Chapter 10)* enabled U.S. advisors to protect themselves from enemy attacks.

In the CINCLANTFLT environment I had to find a way to provide Captain Hibbs a means of coaching U.S. surveillance assets (submarines, P3 aircraft, SOSUS) onto the approximate location of the deploying nuclear-propelled *Yankee*-class Soviet ballistic missile submarine. It was vital that we learn their patrol stations and devise a means of trailing them.

However, a look at the command environment in 1969

(according to my somewhat fallible memory) indicates that the world was basically divided into three Unified Commands: CINCPAC, CINCLANT, and CINCEUR. The four-star Admiral who served as CINCLANT (commanding all Army, Navy, Air Force, and Marines in the Atlantic Command) was also CINCLANTFLT (Commander in Chief U.S. Atlantic Fleet) and SACLANT (Supreme Allied Commander Atlantic), which was the NATO (North Atlantic Treaty Organization) commander.

Operational Commanders under CINCLANTFLT included COM2ndFLT and COMASWFORLANT. As such, they had NATO "hats" as well and COMASWFORLANT's NATO command was COMOCEANSLANT.

There were also under CINCLANTFLT major type commanders: COMSUBLANT, COMNAVAIRLANT, and COMNAVSURFLANT. They were responsible for the training and upkeep of their submarines, aircraft and aircraft carriers, and surface forces respectively. As ships completed overhaul and refresher training to become further qualified, they were "chopped" to one of the operating commanders for operations. Thus, COMASWFORLANT might at any given time be exercising operational control over an ASW aircraft carrier with Carrier Air Group embarked, or a squadron of P3 Orion ASW patrol aircraft, and be coordinating operations among ASW submarines, destroyers, and P3s.

If the reader is now thoroughly confused, imagine how confusing it was to work at the command level in such an environment.

In late 1969 a Soviet "*Yankee*-class" ballistic missile submarine departed her base in the North Sea and was detected by our SOSUS arrays passing through the waters off Iceland. Our P3 squadron began tracking the submarine using magnetic anomaly detectors (MAD gear) and sonobuoys.

Handing off tracking to USS *Lapon* (SSN 661), a nuclear attack submarine of the *Sturgeon* class, we continued to track the Soviet ship. Commander Chester "Whitey" Mack, skipper of the *Lapon*, had earlier employed the ship in exercises that demonstrated the feasibility of trailing another submarine. This procedure called for consummate skill in avoiding the numerous tactics employed by the Soviet to break trail if it was suspected that there was a trailing submarine. *Lapon* tailed the *Yankee* for 47 days of the *Yankee*'s transit and patrol (off the coast of Bermuda), breaking contact when the *Yankee* turned and headed home. *Lapon* was awarded a Presidential Unit Citation for this feat.

But that wasn't the whole story. On two occasions *Lapon* lost the trail. In each case, P3 aircraft out of Lajes and Bermuda respectively, were coached on to the *Yankee* by means of special intelligence that I was able to make available to Captain Hibbs. They re-established contact and successfully turned the Soviet over to *Lapon* who continued the trail.

Hibbs and I made an inseparable team after that and we were affectionately (and occasionally jealously) termed "Abie's Irish Rose" (many readers will have to "Google" this to determine the reference); however, it suffices to say that our show went on uninterrupted for many months. In fact, the Admirals and Generals based in the big cave under a mountain in Colorado, known as NORAD, requested a briefing – and Al and I were designated to go. What a thrill to board an Air Force version of the Lear jet, piloted by two "bird" colonels. We were given the full VIP treatment and, upon arrival in Colorado, I caught up with my old Vietnam buddy, Steve Samuels (now LCOL Samuels), who gave us a great tour of the Air Force Academy and treated us to a steak dinner of heroic proportions. The reflected glare of stars from the uniforms of the twelve General and Flag officers attending did not interfere with our briefing, and our Lear jet flight back to Oceana Naval Air Station was uneventful.

Vice Admiral Masterton "liked my style" and recommended I be promoted to Captain two years ahead of my year group.

ANNABEL AND I bought a four-wheel-drive Toyota Land Cruiser and went camping on the Outer Banks of North Carolina. As demanding as my job was, after five years of arduous duty, family time was overdue and we were determined to make the most of it. I had a box constructed to fit on top of the Cruiser into which we stuffed tent, screen house, cots, rafts, surfboard, lanterns and stove. Into the back went Judy, now a typical 16-year-old, Skip, now 14, and coolers of food and drinks. We set up camp at the Hatteras Island Campground and spent a couple of great weekends surfing, fishing, swimming, eating and playing Scrabble. Skip learned how to surf. On the way home Annabel said, "I really liked that. Let's get a house at the beach."

ON JULY 1, 1970, Radm. Elmo R. Zumwalt, Jr. was promoted over the heads of 92 senior flag officers to be Chief of Naval Operations (CNO). He is famous for issuing a serious of directives called "Z-grams" designed to transform the Navy and make a Navy career more appealing. The arrival of a new CNO creates considerable rotation in senior flag officer assignments as the new boss puts his team in place. Before too long, Vice Adm. Masterton received a visit from the Vice CNO advising him that he was slated for retirement. At the time there were only 23 Vice Adm. positions in the Navy. In 1971 he was relieved as COMASWFORLANT by Vice Adm. Fred Bennett, formerly Commandant of the Naval War College.

Admiral Bennett had suffered a heart attack but was sufficiently recovered to remain on active duty. Whereas Admiral Masterton spent most non-business lunch hours playing squash with his aide, Admiral Bennett hustled over to the Fleet Recreation Park to get in a good swim. Al Hibbs and I frequently joined him. Perks for three-star admirals were being nibbled away. For example, Bennett lived in one of the grand old mansions on the Naval Station that had been built for the Jamestown Exposition of 1907 – but he was not permitted to be driven by his Navy driver in his official sedan from his quarters to his office two miles away. He had to drive his own car to the office and then use the official car for business trips during the day, returning home in his own car. It was difficult to imagine an executive with his responsibilities not being driven to and from work in a company limo. In any event, Al Hibbs or I usually drove the Admiral to and from our swimming sessions.

I mentioned the P3 ASW and Surveillance aircraft used

A SPECIAL OPERATION

In early 1972 Commander in Chief U. S. Atlantic Fleet (CINCLANTFLT) staffers queried Commander Anti-Submarine Forces Atlantic (COMASWFORLANT) as to the feasibility of pursuing a bilateral agreement with the Royal Netherlands Navy (RNN) that would permit Navy P3 *Orion* aircraft under the operational control of COMAS-WFORLANT to land and refuel in South America in order to conduct surveillance operations in the South Atlantic.

The Soviet Navy's enhanced ability to conduct blue water operations had been demonstrated in the late 1960s when a Soviet naval task force suddenly appeared in South Atlantic waters. The ASW force commander, after involved negotiation with British authorities, dispatched a P3 aircraft to the Ascension Islands with orders to conduct reconnaissance on the Soviet units. Our aircrew found minimal support there, slept under the wing of their aircraft and dealt with a myriad of communications problems. However, they were unable to receive basic intelligence support, including area weather information, while on the ground. COMASWFORLANT, had specific responsibilities in the South Atlantic under his NATO hat as Commander in the trailing of the *Yankee*-class SSBN. This aircraft which came into service in the Navy in 1962 and, at the time of this writing (2012) has been in continuous use for 50 years, is in the process of being phased out by the new Poseidon aircraft. The P3 was a militarized version of the Lockheed Electra airliner, powered by four turbo-prop engines. Turbo-prop is somewhat misunderstood; it is a pure jet engine used to power a propeller. These aircraft went though several iterations, usually due to technological upgrades. Thus, when the new P3C came along

South Atlantic (COMSOLANT).

A special operation was set in motion to test whether P3 aircraft could operate out of Surinam (formerly Dutch Guiana) utilizing a World War II era landing strip originally built for Naval Air Transport Service (NATS) and subsequently Military Air Transport Service (MATS) flights. CINCLANTFLT, in his CINCLANT hat, would work through his State Department representative to establish communications from fleet headquarters in Norfolk through the State Department to the U.S. consular office in Paramaribo.

As COMASWFORLANT Assistant Chief of Staff, Intelligence, I and Captain Al Hibbs, Current Operations Officer, were charged with conducting the actual operational feasibility test. Hibbs and I, along with my Royal Netherlands Navy (RNN) NATO counterpart, departed NAS Norfolk for Curaçao on a P3B provided by COMNAVAIRLANT. In Curaçao we were treated royally by our RNN hosts and the U.S. Consul who, when briefed, were eager to cooperate in our mission.

From Curaçao we flew on to Surinam. Approaching from the sea, we flew low over the jungle to a smooth landing on a virtually deserted airstrip. A jeep approached

sporting a new computerized tracking and analysis system, Al Hibbs and I were invited by COMNAVAIRLANT to fly in one from Norfolk to Keflavic, Iceland (a NATO airbase) and return. It was my first visit to Iceland and Al and I had a blast. An intelligence colleague of mine, Lt. Charlie Chitty, and his wife gave us the royal tour of Reykjavik and in this land of the midnight sun we bought Icelandic wool sweaters for the whole family, sheepskin rugs and quart jars of caviar. Judy and Skip's bedrooms smelled like lamb chops for months.

carrying a Guianian in khaki attire who managed to convey to us, in a combination of halting English and sign language, that he had been advised by telephone to expect our arrival. He showed us where we could fuel the aircraft, identified an abandoned barracks where the crew could set up camp, affirmed that he would drive the three of us to Paramaribo that afternoon, wait overnight, and take us back to the airport the next morning. Our hour-long ride to the city afforded us a view of primitive huts out of which whole families appeared and lined the road to watch us pass. Often, the presumed head of family stood with breechcloth, spear, and shield, waving the spear in greeting while unclothed children jumped up and down excitedly.

The hotel room was spacious, not air-conditioned, and very hot and steamy. We relaxed, poured a libation and sat in our skivvies waiting for the results of the intelligence link we hoped had been established. Presently, there was knock on the door. I opened it and admitted the Consular Office representative, who looked like a character from a John leCarré spy novel in a wrinkled white suit and Panama hat. "Captain Hibbs?" he asked. Al, trying to look as dignified as possible in his undershorts, identified himself. "I have a SECRET

IN THE SPRING of 1971, with a little help from Annabel's family and with every penny we could scrape up, we built a 1,200-foot, three-bedroom beach cottage in the Sandbridge area of Virginia Beach. Sandbridge, the Virginia origins of the outer banks of North Carolina, is a narrow strip of land extending from the southern end of Virginia Beach to the North Carolina border less than twelve miles south. Flanked by the Atlantic Ocean on one side and a series of bays on the other side, the cottage, enlarged on a couple of occasions, has been a major marshalling point for over

message for you," continued our visitor, handing an envelope to Hibbs. He then joined us for refreshment, told us where we could find a good restaurant for dinner, and departed.

The envelope contained a message from the Fleet Commander, forwarded through State Department channels. It ordered us to depart at 0800 hours, conduct a surface surveillance patrol in the area bounded by specific coordinates, and advised that there was no indication of any sub-surface activity in the area but to be prepared to drop sonobuoys if directed. The message then gave the area weather forecast and directed the pilot to secure the search and return to base when ordered by Capt. Hibbs.

Our jeep ride back to the airstrip was uneventful as were our flight to the op area, our search within, and our return to Norfolk. It had been sufficiently demonstrated that with a little juggling we could put airborne resources into the South Atlantic for a limited period until surface and/or sub-surface forces could be deployed. A bilateral agreement was drafted and executed between U.S. and Netherlands CINCs. For all I know. it has never been abrogated and remains in effect to this day buried in some forgotten archive. ★

Al Hibbs

40 years – for children, grandchildren, and now a great-grandchild.

A ROUTINE VISIT to my detailer at the Bureau of Naval Personnel in Washington brought good news and some news to reflect upon. "You will be selected for Captain in the Fall and will be ordered to a Captain's billet at the Pentagon even before your promotion comes through. I have every confidence, based on your tour in command and your fitness reports at ASWFORLANT, that you will screen for a major command and be ordered back to sea in about three years," he said.

I felt pretty good because detailers are notoriously reluctant to make any promises. Nevertheless, I fully intended to remain on active duty as long as the Navy would have me. There were some gray clouds in the picture, however. Annabel's career at Old Dominion University seemed secure. Our high-school-aged children were doing very well and the thought of moving to Washington and leaving Sandbridge was not appealing. Some of my friends in the same situation left their families in Norfolk and moved to D.C. with plans to commute home on weekends. Things didn't always work out as planned. In the first place, Pentagon duty was in no way a 9AM-5PM, 40-hour week. For many it was more like 5AM-9PM, six-and-a-half days a week. They were lucky to get home once a month. Family ties were strained, in some cases to the breaking point.

Just as Annabel and I were thinking this over, Ed Snyder, president of Checkered Flag Motor Car Company, and I had lunch together. His dealership sold Jaguar, MG automobiles and Honda motorcycles as well as Toyota, "the new car from

Japan". Ed was getting ready to build an exclusive dealership for Toyota in Virginia Beach and needed a general manager at the "mother store."

"Why don't you leave the Navy and come to work for me?" he asked. Other than being a car enthusiast, "What do I know about the car business?" I replied. Ed said, "You make a good appearance; I know you know how to work with people; and I don't think you will steal from me. I can teach you the rest."

The chance to earn considerably more than what I was making in the Navy, plus the opportunity of not uprooting my family, was tempting; but giving up a promotion and the chance to command a cruiser or a squadron of destroyers was very difficult to consider. After weeks of sleepless nights and with my family's assurance that they were with me whichever way I went, I elected to retire from the Navy, twenty years to the day after I entered Officer Candidate School.

I NEVER LOOKED BACK. I loved the Navy for twenty years, yet never regretted my decision. Happily for me, in later years I was reunited with shipmates at various reunions and was able to take great pride in the accomplishments of my men and officers.

"I can imagine no more rewarding a career. And any man who may be asked in this century what he did to make his life worthwhile, I think can respond with a good deal of satisfaction: I served in the United States Navy."

– *John F. Kennedy, 1963*

United States Atlantic Fleet
Headquarters of the Commander in Chief

The President of the United States takes pleasure in presenting the

MERITORIOUS SERVICE MEDAL to

COMMANDER HAROLD H. SACKS

UNITED STATES NAVY

for service as set forth in the following

CITATION:

For outstandingly meritorious service from 20 August 1969 to 31 August 1972 while serving as Assistant Chief of Staff for Intelligence, Commander Antisubmarine Warfare Force, U. S. Atlantic Fleet. Displaying outstanding leadership, planning and managerial abilities, and resourcefulness, Commander SACKS initiated major programs which improved the intelligence capabilities of the Force and provided valuable support within the Atlantic Fleet operational and intelligence communities. His diligent efforts in formulating significant bilateral agreements contributed measurably to the evolution of multinational antisubmarine warfare cooperation. By his outstanding performance and inspiring devotion to duty, Commander SACKS upheld the highest traditions of the United States Naval Service.

For the President

CHARLES K. DUNCAN
Admiral, U. S. Navy
Commander in Chief U. S. Atlantic Fleet

Meritorious Service Medal citation.

★

AFTERWORD

OVER A QUARTER CENTURY passed after my retirement without my giving a great deal of thought to the Navy. I had friends who bought homes overlooking the Thimble Shoals Channel and watched Navy vessels passing in and out of port; they went to every change of command ceremony and launching they could attend. That was not my style at the time. I was busy educating children, pursuing multiple careers, and then watching my children become married adults and parents.

Then one day I received a phone call from Harold Craft, who was 19 years old when he was seaman apprentice aboard *Steinaker*. Harold had been my driver and, since we spent time together off the ship, I got to know him pretty well and was even able to help him resolve some personal issues. "Captain Sacks," he said, "The USS *Steinaker* Association is having a reunion in Virginia Beach this summer. I and my wife Linda would drive up from South Carolina if we thought you would be there." I had previously no thought whatsoever of participating in this event; however, Craft seemed so hopeful that I agreed to meet them at the oceanfront hotel in which the reunion was held. We had a pretty good time despite the fact that I knew none of the attendees besides Harold Craft. The attendees were mostly from years preceding my tour aboard *Steinaker*. But it was special and a bit humbling seeing Harold and meeting his lovely wife Linda. Harold told me that his mother so appreciated my communications to the families of the crew during the Vietnam deployment that she displayed my photograph on her kitchen wall until she passed away. Subsequently, we went to another Steinaker Association reunion together but I had little success

Front row, from the left: Harold Craft, Cary Beach, John Ives,
Walt Hummel, Hal Sacks, Bob Doyle, Hugh Carroll, Bob Patton,
Chris Horsch, Bill Raub, and Tom Simcoe
Charleston, SC 2011

convincing officers from my time aboard the ship to attend and
my only link with most of the attendees was that at one time or
another we had all served on the same ship.

Some years passed and again I received a phone call from
Harold Craft. "Captain Sacks," he said, "Would you be willing
to come to Mobile, Alabama this summer and meet with a few
of us who deployed to Vietnam with you?"

"You bet I would," was my immediate reply. Annabel was
at first less than enthusiastic about the trip, protesting that she
really didn't know any of the enlisted men and, since not many
of them were married at the time, she didn't know their wives
either. However, the "Navy wife" in her surfaced and off we went
to be met at the Mobile airport by Harold and Chuck Harrell. To
put it simply, we had a wonderful time. Annabel loved meeting
and becoming friends with SK3 Cary Beach and wife Lyn; SM2

Chuck Harrell and wife Roberta; SM3 Tom Simcoe and wife Barbara; SN Bill Raub and wife Carol, RD3 Sam Reason, PN Greg Brown, and RD John Ives. We toured and had lunch in the wardroom of the USS *Alabama* (BB60) and began a tradition that would get us together about every two years since. Our group has greatly expanded thanks to the work of Bob Patton who gathered many of the wardroom officers into the fold.

MY YOUNG AND LEAN seamen and junior officers are mostly grandparents themselves, no longer so young and not so lean. We have since met in Norfolk, VA; Philadelphia, PA; Williamsburg, VA; Baton Rouge, LA; Charleston, SC; and Washington, DC. Over the past years, several have developed illnesses due to exposure to Agent Orange, a poisonous herbicide used during the Vietnam War. As their Captain, I have had an additional duty to verify their service in the war zone in order that they might receive treatment and compensation from the Veterans Administration. Sometimes we have had great results. A typical letter follows:

CDR. HAROLD H. SACKS, USN (RET)

530 BOISSEVAIN AVENUE NORFOLK, VA 23507

June 7, 2012

SM2 Edward Sauer
1011 North 24th Street
Billings, Montana 59101

Dear Ed,

This is to confirm that you served with me in USS Steinaker *(DD863) in 1968. I was the Commanding Officer and you served in the Operations Department during the ship's deployment to Vietnam, as Signalman (SM2). The ship was assigned to the 7th Fleet from 20 May through 1 October 1968 and participated in the following operations: Naval Gunfire Support (NGFS) missions off Binh Thuan and Phu Yen Provinces; "Sea Dragon" operations off the coast of North Vietnam to interdict seaborne infiltration of Communist forces into South Vietnam; and antiaircraft picket duty off the demilitarized zone. We also operated with aircraft carriers conducting strikes against North Vietnam.*

On occasion during this deployment, you accompanied me ashore in the Republic of Vietnam. In particular, I recall our mission ashore in Phan Thiet, III Corps on August 10 of 1968. The Vietnamese province chief, in appreciation of our effective shore bombardment there, awarded us the Vietnamese Cross of Gallantry. Along with the ship's crew you were also awarded the Combat Operations Medal.

You joined me in supporting our Junk Forces in Phan Thiet and assisted Lt. (jg) Beckett, the Communications Officer, in coordinating surveillance and communication procedures with Vietnamese nationals in the Junk Force. If you require any further information regarding your service during this deployment, please feel free to contact me.

I hereby certify that the information I have provided is true to the best of my knowledge and belief.

In the meantime, I and your shipmates wish you every success in obtaining the benefits you have earned.

Sincerely,
Cdr. Harold H. Sacks USN (Ret)
135-24-4124

ONE SHIPMATE had suffered from Parkinson's disease for seventeen years while waiting for help from the Veterans Administration. The letter finally got their attention and he now has the help he needs and, although in a wheelchair, has been able to attend our reunions. He wrote:

> *Capt. Hal: I want you to know that I have been granted 100% disability in conjunction with Agent Orange while in Vietnam and I thank you from the bottom of my heart for the letter you sent on my behalf…Walt Hummel QM1 USN RET.*

TO CLOSE THIS MEMOIR, I have saved one last story told by Cary Beach at our first reunion in Mobile. The incident had completely slipped my memory. In Cary's words:

> *September 30, 1968 was our last day on the gunline. When relieved we would proceed to Subic Bay, load provisions and head for home. Shortly before midnight the Captain entered the Combat Information Center (CIC) and announced that all voice communications were inoperative.*
>
> *"But Captain," the radarmen answered, "we are hearing everyone loud and clear and our relief has been calling us – 'Tomboy (our voice call), Tomboy, we are enroute and are ready to relieve you.'"*
>
> *"You may monitor but may not reply," the Captain ordered, "until we complete one more fire mission."*
>
> *"Aye, aye sir," the radarmen replied.*
>
> *Twenty minutes later, at approximately 0010, October 1, 1968, the Captain entered the CIC and announced, "All voice communications are now restored. You may report that we stand relieved and are departing the gun-line."*

Apparently, I had managed to keep the ship firing until the first of October, thus qualifying the entire crew for an additional month's combat pay. It was only $65 (tax-free), but a substantial sum to seaman in 1968.

ANNABEL AND I look forward to future reunions.

**Retired U.S. Navy Captains Bob Patton,
Bob (Willie) Williams, Hugh Carroll**
June 8, 2013

★

APPENDIX

Excerpts From The Captain's Log
USS *Steinaker* (DD863)

W HEN USS *STEINAKER* (DD-863) sailed for duty in the Vietnam conflict, one of the greatest morale problems faced by the Commanding Officer was the inability to establish good communications between the ship's sailors and their loved ones. There was no e-mail, no video conferencing, and only in the rare case of an emergency was it possible to send what was termed a "Class Easy" message (in reality, a telegram). The Captain of the ship, the "Old Man," was 38 years old, his second-in-command barely 30. The rest of the officers averaged 26 years of age and two-thirds of the enlisted sailors were 19 or younger. Mail was considered excellent when letters arrived a mere ten days after being sent, but it was clear that letters crossed and families faced many frustrations, having to make decisions without timely interaction with the "man of the house."

These young men did not always realize how important it was to parents, wives, children, and sweethearts to receive mail, and to learn what was going on in the ship. During the Korean conflict, for example, the ship I served in, USS *Owen* (DD-536) received minor damage from a shore battery projectile. Radio Moscow reported the ship was sunk, which misinformation was picked up by the *New York Times* and read by wives and families before the Navy was able to notify them that we were indeed safe.

Even when motivated to write home, many of the young men were somewhat inarticulate. Thus, the idea of a typewritten brief sheet, copied on the shipboard "ditto" machine, and placed in the mess decks for the men to stuff into their letters seemed appropriate to keep families informed. The title, "Excerpts from the Captain's Log," seemed suitable; each "Excerpt" was written by the Captain and, so titled, also had the ring of authenticity. In due course I was the recipient of dozens of notes from parents and wives expressing their gratitude for these periodic pieces.

From time to time the ship mailed a longer letter to next of kin and a sampling is included here. In these times of professional family organizations and easy daily communications between sailors and loved ones it is perhaps of interest to recall the efforts made three decades ago to keep in touch.

January, 2002   Commander Harold H. Sacks, USN (ret)

History of the USS *Steinaker* (DD 863)

THE USS *STEINAKER* is a FRAM I *Gearing*-(DD–710)-class destroyer. She was built by the Bethlehem Steel Company in Staten Island, New York, and commissioned on 26 May 1945. The ship is named in honor of Private First Class Donald Daur Steinaker, United States Marine Corps Reserve, who was killed at the age of 20 during the early campaign for Guadalcanal.

As a member of the First Raider Battalion, *Steinaker* participated in a violent battle against overwhelming Japanese forces during the morning of 8 October 1942. Fifty-nine Japanese were killed in the battle that took the lives of twelve marines. Private Steinaker refused to leave his position and died heroically defending it. For this action he was posthumously awarded the Navy Cross.

In 1952, *Steinaker* was decommissioned and entered the yards for conversion to a USS *Eugene Greene*-(DDR-711)-class Radar Picket Destroyer. When recommissioned in 1953, she was fitted with the latest early warning radar for use in long-range detection of enemy aircraft. *Steinaker* was again converted in 1964 under the Fleet Rehabilitation and Modernization (FRAM) Program. As a FRAM Mark 1 destroyer, *Steinaker* carried highly sophisticated and modern anti-submarine weapons and detection equipment, including Drone Antisubmarine Helicopters (DASH) and Nuclear Depth Bomb-armed Antisubmarine Rockets (ASROC). This capability, combined with modern radar and five-inch gun mounts, rendered *Steinaker* one of the most versatile ships in the United States Fleet.

Prior to conversion, *Steinaker* was attached to Destroyer Squadron 26, for which she served as Flagship in 1959, 1961, and 1962. In 1962 she was awarded the Destroyer Squadron 26 Battle Efficiency "E." Upon completion of the FRAM I conversion *Steinaker* joined Destroyer Squadron 2 in Norfolk on 24 April 1965, and a month later celebrated her 20th anniversary during refresher training at Guantánamo Bay, Cuba.

During fifteen Mediterranean deployments, *Steinaker* had numerous operations with NATO and Sixth Fleet Forces and in 1967 served two months in the Red Sea and Indian Ocean as a unit of the Middle East Force. *Steinaker* has shown the American Flag in ports from Northern Europe to India.

The Cold War period saw *Steinaker* participate in a myriad of operations. In 1949 she participated in cold weather operations off the coast of Nova Scotia and in 1953 she took part in Operation Mariner. In July and August 1958 *Steinaker* operated with the Sixth Fleet in support of U.S. Marine landings in Lebanon. She was attached to the Project Mercury

Space Program during April 1961 and was called upon to assume blockade duties during the Cuban Missile Crisis in 1962. In October and November 1967 she served as a Missile Range Instrumentation Ship under the operational control of Commander Submarine Force, U.S. Atlantic Fleet during test firings of the Poseidon ballistic missile. A brief training cruise in early 1968 was used to sharpen *Steinaker's* operational capability prior to her deployment to the Pacific.

30 March 1968

Excerpts from the Captain's Log #1

En route Panama Canal from Norfolk, Virginia

OUR DEPARTURE FROM NORFOLK was in sunshine. Leaving homeport for a major deployment is generally thought of as a gray day, but despite tearful goodbyes there was almost a sense of relief aboard ship – relief from the intense preparations which really began in December, and from the somewhat tense days we all experienced just before leaving our families.

Just prior to getting underway, the following prayer was offered over the ship's announcement system:

> *Almighty God, we turn our thoughts to thee as we make ready to sail for distant places. Thou knowest the future and will defend us from all adversities both to the soul and body if we fully trust in thee. Enable each of us to cheerfully accept his respective place of duty within the ship that we may pass all our days in devotion to our sacred tasks. Watch over our wives, children, and loved ones at*

home through all the days of our separation, that our
return may be a blessed homecoming. Grant us a good
ship's spirit, a happy voyage, and a safe return. Amen.

The transit to Panama began in very smooth seas, which, as the days passed, grew a bit rougher and some of the men had a chance to try out their sea legs. One of the more experienced men took sick and the Task Unit diverted from its course to stop briefly at the harbor entrance to Guantánamo Bay, Cuba, where he was transferred by boat to the Naval Hospital there.

Steinaker's most important accomplishment on this leg of our journey was the satisfactory completion of a full power run, designed to put our boilers and machinery to the test. I was gratified that all the hard work put into the plant by our engineers paid off – and we view the future with increased confidence in

First Row: Eggart, Auberry, Kahn, Hutchins, Costea, Stone, BMC, LTJG Patton Second Row: Coty, Grove, Vest, Price, Littman, Dallas, Craft, Gaijan Third Row: Ryan, Reeley, Beaulieu, Clark, Fulton, Griswald, Sheety, Wiktorowski, Meldola, Bischoff, Angell Fourth Row: Fadely, Rouse, Jackson, Brown, Raub, Macleod, Orr, Carducci, Blazie, Connor Fifth Row: French, Miller, Pettigrew, Cave

our ability to get there, get the job done, and get back.

For most of us the fact that this will be such a long deployment has not yet fully registered. It is hard to believe that we won't be turning for home in a few weeks. Our first mail from home, in Panama, will doubtless serve to remind us otherwise.

7 April 1968

Excerpts From The Captain's Log #2

Enroute San Diego, California From Panama Canal

OUR SPIRITS DAMPENED only slightly by the fact that civil disturbances in Panama itself would restrict shore leave; the passage through the locks was fascinating as ever. It is difficult to believe that this is an operation run totally without cost to the American taxpayer, yet the price of transit for ships hasn't been increased since 1918. For the crew it was practically an "all hands on deck with cameras" evolution, except during the passage through Gatun Lake, when bathing suits were in order as the crew took advantage of the fresh water to flush all water systems and scrub the ship down from top to bottom with fresh water, a luxury indeed for men-o-war. I couldn't help but think back nostalgically to my first transit of the canal, on my first naval cruise to Korean waters over fifteen years ago. Looking at the eager young men about the ship, I wondered if their thoughts were the same as mine had been.

The transit from Panama to San Diego is a long haul for a destroyer, but the weather has been as close to perfect as possible and the time has been well spent, training, working on some of our secondary but still important upkeep items which took a back seat during our frenetic pre-overseas maintenance (POM) period.

On the spur of the moment, just the day before leaving Norfolk, we purchased a slot-car racetrack kit and stocked additional cars and car-kits in the ship's store. Within a few hours after payday every car in the store was sold, and each evening the would-be Gran Prix racers have been driving the slots, the Captain included.

Today, Sunday at sea, has been mostly holiday routine: brunch, lay services, and a movie matinee; a fitting end to a busy week during which our DASH (Drone Anti-Submarine Helicopter) team made us all quite proud by their distinguished performance.*

Mail was quite sparse in Panama, but we expect a real haul in San Diego.

* The DASH team kept at least one "bird" in the air 24 hours a day for six days and nights, establishing an Atlantic Fleet record unchallenged to this day.

16 April 1968

Excerpts From The Captain's Log #3

Enroute Pearl Harbor, Hawaii From San Diego, California

WE ARRIVED AT SAN DIEGO almost simultaneously with the worst earth tremor experienced in Southern California in over a decade, followed by a classic "Santa Ana," a weather anomaly characterized by two to three days of hot, dry air (temperatures unseasonably high in the high 80s and on one day reaching 90). The evenings were quite cool. Neither of these interfered with

Front Row: LTJG Spencer, Gilbert, Taylor, Burridge, Schellinger, Chief Banks Second Row: Taylor, Henderson, Kirk, Scott, Recelli, Abramski Third Row: Gilbert, Haynes, Ashley, Pearson, Barre, Hurst, Lomboy

the highly enjoyable tours to Disneyland and the truly remarkable San Diego Zoo. I'm certain that those adventurous souls who felt a visit to Tijuana, Mexico was an absolute must might have agreed that Disneyland was by far the better place to go.*

Our transit got off to a good beginning as we had an opportunity to conduct AA firing exercises the first day out before settling down for the long haul. The weather has been overcast with rather heavy but mostly following seas, thus our progress has been according to schedule.

The USAFI group study program is underway with about 50 men enrolled in college level courses, including: Fundamentals of Business Law, Trigonometry, and Auto Mechanics. We picked up an old auto engine before sailing, which is used for practical work. I wish we had the time and facilities to do even more along this line.

Easter Sunday began with rain, washing out our sunrise

service topside, however, regular services were held later and the day was given over to DASH operations. About one fourth of the crew was able to send radiograms to their families via our ham radio station, and Jewish personnel from *Steinaker, Blandy, Borie* and *Rich* (the rest of our division) gathered in our wardroom to celebrate the Passover festival with the traditional ceremonial meal (*Seder*).

It was a pleasure to present advancement in rating certificates to 35 men who competed successfully in Navy-wide examinations for promotion. For them there will be something extra to celebrate in Hawaii.

*I seem to remember that in 1953, enroute to Korea, I joined a group of junior officers on a never-to-be-forgotten trip to Tijuana. Was there a Disneyland in 1953? Would we have gone?

5 May 1968

Excerpts From The Captain's Log #4

Enroute Subic Bay, Philippine Islands from Pearl Harbor, Hawaii

CAPTAIN JAMES COOK sailed the *Endeavor* into Matavai Bay, Tahiti one hundred ninety years, almost to the day, before *Steinaker* "discovered" Pearl Harbor. If the comparison seems a bit forced, let there be no mistake: our East coast sailors are discovering this part of the world for themselves. For those of us who have not revisited Hawaii in over a decade, the changes are staggering. Despite a heavy schedule of briefings, maintenance, and inspections, the beaches, fine restaurants and clubs were enjoyed.

The short leg to Midway Island, where we made a brief stop for fuel, was a productive one, as *Steinaker* completed the last competitive exercise requirements for the year. Midway remains largely unchanged with crystal clear water, the whitest of sand beaches, and the aptly named, ubiquitous gooney birds. A few cases of chilled beer, a surfside game of touch football, and a refreshing swim made even this brief stop a pleasant interlude for the crew. Our stop at Guam was another matter. Far larger than Midway, with widespread facilities, it was touch and go right up until sailing whether or not all hands would make it back to the ship on time. For myself there was a pleasant reunion with old friends and former shipmates. Our present assignment notwithstanding, *Steinaker*'s primary mission remains Antisubmarine Warfare (ASW), and the opportunity to keep our hand in by exercising with a submarine on departing Guam was

L to R: LTJG Franck (ASWO), Stewart STC. 2nd Row: Pate SN, Baber STG2, McNeely STG2, Sheets STG3, Cook GMG3, Dobbins TM3. 3rd Row: Six SN, Balcom STG2, Gibson GMG2, Davis STG2, Hancock STG3, Welch SN. 4th Row: Vorys STG2, Myers STG2, Demers STG2, Schuchart STG2.

most welcome. That we did well made it all the sweeter.

The past few days have been devoted to some very realistic naval gunfire support training and to the training of our repair parties at damage control. No grim overtones are intended here – it's just a matter of large doses of preventive medicine, in keeping with our announced "game plan" of getting there, getting the job done, and getting back.

Thus, with the historic San Bernardino Straits behind us, our 12,163-mile trek to Subic Bay draws to an end. I'm not sure that the airline motto is applicable here ("getting there is half the fun") but we did it without mishap, and have learned from each other on the way.

24 May 1968

Excerpts From The Captain's Log #5

Subic Bay, Philippine Islands to "Yankee Station," Gulf of Tonkin

SUBIC BAY HAS UNDERGONE a miraculous metamorphosis during the past few years. I know of no support facility in the world where so many top-notch people are working so hard to say "can do" to the Fleet.

We departed Subic for a few days to provide gunfire support training to U.S. Marine spotters on the island of Luzon, not exactly the dramatic role we had hoped to play, but our turn will come and these same marines may be our spotters in the months ahead. Returning to Subic for a very brief stay, we sailed again, this time to escort the USS *Ticonderoga* to Yankee Station and then to join the USS *Bon Homme Richard* (CVA 31) where we are sharing the rescue destroyer chores with our sister ship, USS

Rich (DD 820). It is easy to see why the elderly carrier is called the "Bonny Dick." Sitting behind her on plane guard station, we remain fascinated by the smoothness of her flight operations, despite the heavy schedule she must contend with. One of her rescue helicopters suffered a casualty and settled into the sea, remaining afloat long enough for our rescue team to take off all personnel safely. When we went alongside the carrier to transfer the crew the skipper expressed his thanks and sent over fresh baked apple pies and several gallons of ice cream, enough to provide a treat for our entire crew.

Speaking of elderly ladies, *Steinaker* will be 23 years young this coming Sunday, May 26, and we are hoping for a sufficient respite from operations to do the honors, cake, fantail steak cookout and so forth. The 21-year-old men aboard may look with envy at the new missile ships, and sometimes I myself get to thinking how nice it would be to have a new ship. After fifteen years in ships just like *Steinaker*, however, I have a healthy respect for their firepower and their ability to steam dependably, come what may. One gets a comfortable feeling, as with an old friend. Our early American destroyer is doing just fine.

9 June 1968

Excerpts From The Captain's Log #6

Yankee Station, Gulf of Tonkin to Singapore

OUR FIRST TOUR ON Yankee Station was a successful one; our role, although unspectacular, was carried off without any hitches, and after a brief stop at Subic we headed for Singapore.

Still in company with "Bonny Dick," our sister ship *Rich*,

Gosnell EN1, Wyhlidko ADR1, Edwards ETN3, Larson ADJ3, Cluen ATC, Carr AN, Spencer LTJG

and joined by USS *Mullany* (DD-528) we moored alongside the piers at HMNB Singapore, deeply saddened by the events of the preceding week. The loss with all hands of our nuclear attack submarine, *Scorpion*, and the assassination of Senator Robert Kennedy has cast a pall over our visit. The British and Australian ships in harbor have conformed to our half-masting of the colors, except on the occasion of the official birthday of the Queen, when all ships were full dressed.

It is hard to believe that in a few years the British Navy will leave this base, this very beautiful base which reflects good care for 150 years.

Singapore Town itself, with its polyglot, friendly peoples, their colorful dress and festivals, has remained as always a place to just relax and be comfortable, shop, and have a good time.

We are ready to return to Yankee Station.

3 July 1968

Excerpts From The Captain's Log #7

Singapore to Yankee Station

ENROUTE TO YANKEE STATION we made a brief sojourn into the domain of King Neptune, crossing the equator on 12 June. Only thirty Shellbacks were aboard, approximately ten percent of the crew, including the captain, the only officer Shellback aboard. The inevitable Pollywog Revolt was bravely withstood, and with the assistance of Davy Jones and the Royal Family suitable revenge was taken during the initiation ceremony.

Our first period during this tour on Yankee Station was spent in support of USS *Enterprise* (CVA(N)-65). At first we had some doubts as to our ability to keep up with the huge nuclear powered ship, but as it turned out we had no problems and it was a pleasure to work with her. Between brief periods in support of "Bonny Dick" we managed to squeeze in some anti-submarine training as one of a group of what has been aptly named, "Musical Destroyers," by our Task Group Commander, who has had to arrange for shuffling us back and forth while retaining sufficient assets with the CVAs. Two days of intensive refresher work were climaxed by a successful exercise torpedo firing. Good to know we haven't lost our touch.

Steinaker is now patrolling an anti-aircraft picket station in the vicinity of the Demilitarized Zone (DMZ), providing early warning to Yankee Station units in the event of hostile intrusion. At night are seen and heard the flashes and explosions of airdropped and ship-fired ordnance, and the occasional pattern of AAA firing from the ground.

In a few days we rejoin "Bonny Dick" to escort her to Subic and then Hong Kong.

Plan of the Day for Crossing the Equator

12 June 1968

UNIFORM FOR POLLYWOGS: t-shirts and dungaree trousers on back-wards (without scivvies), shower shoes

1130 – All royal shellbacks meeting in the hangar deck

1200 – All pollywogs assemble on the forecastle, commence saltwater washdown.

1215 – Neptunis Rex arriving. Pass over 1mc with 8 bells.

1230 – Break Jolly Roger flag – Hummel QM1

1230 – Commence ceremony when commanded by King Neptune

1630 – Mess gear

1645 – Supper for pollywogs supervised by shellbacks

1715 – Supper for shellbacks* mess cooks Ens. Horsch and Ens. Patton

Special Cases

• Lt. (jg) Williams: dressed in old clothes on backwards with white hat and hot caseman gloves counting beans (just fwd of signal bridge sitting on 863).

• Lt. (jg) Beckett: in the eye of the ship with corn broom overhead. Looking for the equator, saying "beep beep." Uniform: Old clothes on backwards.

• Lt. (jg) Conroy: holding two chart tubes for binoculars (stuffed with onions), helping Lt. (jg) Beckett find the equator. Uniform: old clothes on backwards and inside out.

• Lt. Comdr. Palmer: to be informed.

Front: Poppe First Row: Cain, Saltzman, McCarvel, Cortese, Fearneyhough, Brod Second Row: Wood, Shellman, Saur, Mowery, Erland, Blankenship, Lewis Third Row: Harrell, Creig, Massengill, Paugh, Gans Fourth Row: Kaufman, Cunningham, Simcoe, Anderson, Chief Krone, LTJG Becket

Route to be followed by Pollywogs: Leave fo'c'sl one at a time on hands and knees; proceed down port side to fantail. King Neptune and court will be on fantail. When through with royal court proceed as directed by King Neptune. Watch reliefs will go first through the initiation.

Attest, for the King,
Davy Jones, Scribe

23 July 1968

Excerpts From The Captain's Log #8

Yankee Station to Subic to Hong Kong to Yankee Station

ON 6 JULY *STEINAKER* FIRED her guns in anger for the first time in her 23 years of service, in response to intense hostile fire from North Vietnamese gun emplacements. About 25 rounds were received, a few of which were much too close for comfort. As a ship was in a high condition of readiness she was able to giver a good account of self while maneuvering clear. For all but a handful of men aboard this was a new experience, however all hands concerned went about their duties in a professional manner. The atmosphere aboard ship was one of relief, that there were no injuries, nor any damage to the ship, and one of newly found self-confidence – a confidence I have always felt regarding this fine crew.

The visits to Subic and Hong Kong were profitable and most enjoyable, particularly for the Captain and three officers who were able to meet their wives in port. Mixed with the incomparable pleasure of such a rendezvous is a measure of guilt – as such a reunion was not possible for others. In Subic, a work party of *Steinaker* men engaged in a people-to-people project, assisting the men of a small village on the Bataan Peninsula to paint their new schoolhouse, while in Hong Kong a group of orphan children were hosted on board. So much for the enjoyment; the profitable part largely involves the merchants at the Hong Kong China Fleet Store. All hands were awaiting the next payday with empty pockets. Hong Kong remains one of the two or three most fabulous spots on this earth – a mind-boggling feast of sightseeing, first-rate hotels, gourmet cuisine, and wonderful shopping.

We returned to Yankee Station with *Bon Homme Richard* and after a brief stint of rescue destroyer work with her and the USS *America* (CVA 66) were ordered to our now familiar anti-aircraft picket station in the vicinity of the Demilitarized Zone (DMZ), where we relieved our temporary sister ship, the USS *Lowry* (DD 770).

9 August

For Immediate Release on Board USS *Steinaker* (DD 863) in the Gulf of Tonkin

DESTROYER SQUADRON TWO Chaplain, Lt. William E. Wilcox CHC, USNR, currently riding this Norfolk-based destroyer, and Chaplain Paul F. Brady, from the Attack Carrier USS *Intrepid* (CVA 11), returned to their base ships today after a whirlwind two-day tour of four Seventh Fleet destroyers stationed several miles off the coast of North Vietnam, about 60 miles southeast of Hanoi. The Protestant-Catholic chaplain team conducted Mass and Communion services aboard each ship they visited and provided individual counseling services. Chaplain Wilcox commented that he felt something like a country circuit rider out of the American West in the 1800s, but his means of transportation was anything but 19th century. Traveling from fantail to fantail via jet-powered Navy logistic helicopters, the chaplains covered over 300 miles in their 25-hour journey. One leg of this journey was accomplished by manila highline. The four ships visited by the chaplains are assigned aircraft search-and-rescue missions, providing valuable insurance for the pilots returning from strike missions. These relatively remote units receive less frequent mail, fuel, and other services normally provided to the ships of the Seventh Fleet. Visits of chaplains to these remote ships are infrequent, but still a vital part of the Navy chaplains' duties in helping to bring religious guidance a little closer to Navy men, no matter where they are stationed.

August 9, 1968

For Immediate Release on Board USS *Steinaker* (DD 863) in the Gulf of Tonkin

FIREMAN RUSSELL GRAHAM of Alvin, Texas departed this Seventh Fleet destroyer today via helicopter on the first leg of a sad journey home. At the request of the parents of the late Lance Corporal George Allen Alford Jr., USMC, killed in Vietnam on 31 July, Fireman Graham, his lifelong friend, will serve as military escort for the remains of Corporal Alford.

19 August 1968

Excerpts From The Captain's Log #9

Yankee Station to Subic to Kaohsiung, Taiwan to Yokosuka, Japan

OUR FIRST TOUR on the gunline was in support of U.S. Marine forces in Phan Tiet, III Corps. At the end of our mission we were visited by the Vietnamese Province Chief, Colonel Li Loi, who commended the assembled crew. Some of us were able to visit the local Junk Force base.

This tour on Yankee Station was mostly routine, except for the last day when I was invited by Captain Dankworth to join him on board *Bon Homme Richard* for a brief plaque exchanging ceremony. I thoroughly enjoyed the helicopter ride and the opportunity to observe the aircraft recovery cycle from Flight Deck Control. Mechanical difficulties with the helo delayed my return and an unscheduled underway refueling was announced. Having complete confidence in my Executive Officer, Lcdr. Palmer, I signaled to him, "Come alongside at your discretion," and he proceeded to conduct the replenishment in "4.0" fashion, earning a "Well Done!" for *Steinaker* from the C.O. of the oiler. I was treated to a return trip to *Steinaker* via manilla high-line.

We departed Yankee Station just as Tropical Storm Rose was upgraded into Typhoon Rose, a few hours before she blew into the Gulf of Tonkin. Faced with a tight schedule a storm evasion course was set for Subic, south of the Paracel Islands, and we arrived on time without hitting any bumps in the road. It was a

Front Row: LTJG Kochanski, Sanders, Jarmer, Rodgers, Rathjen, Anderson, Chief Richardson Back Row: Johnson, Brown, Henry, Foote

pleasure to have our Commodore, Captain Frank Dunham, from whom we have been separated for over three months, aboard with his staff for lunch, and to receive from him on behalf of Rear Adm. Jack Wadleigh, our Flotilla Commander, our second award for wardroom excellence.

Remaining in Subic only long enough to transfer classified cargo, we hastened to Kaohsiung, where, despite a stay of only a few hours we were able to take advantage of the destroyer tender *Piedmont*'s presence to accomplish certain important work. There was no time for liberty, and *Steinaker*'s East Coast sailors looked longingly across the crowded harbor, to the city they had never visited, and could only wish that our next visit would be a longer one.

Again, fortunate to have missed Tropical Storm Polly completely, we transited uneventfully to Japan through the Shimonoseki Straits. With us was an advance detachment of 25 men from *Piedmont*, mostly repair technicians, who more than earned their keep enroute, and who thoroughly enjoyed their high-speed transportation.

With our special cargo removed we were able to resume DASH ops and volleyball games on our postage-stamp-sized flight deck.

8 September 1968

Excerpts From The Captain's Log #10

Yokosuka, Japan to Tonkin Gulf via Buckner Bay, Okinawa, Tabones Islands, Luzon, and Subic

OUR STAY IN YOKOSUKA was hectic, as maximum advantage was taken of the repair facilities and wonderful opportunities to tour Japan. *Steinaker* entered her 43rd month out of drydock and certain equipment has been operating on borrowed time, however ship's force, with the superb assistance of the Ship's Repair Facility, Yokosuka, completed all the critical work required. I fully expected that *Steinaker*, having gone this far without a significant casualty, would continue to meet all commitments.

Despite a spate of rainy weather, all hands spent their spare time exploring what to most of them was a new world, Japan. Whether heading South to the templed charm of traditional Kyoto, a pilgrimage to Nagasaki or Hiroshima, or North to the slick big city glitter of Tokyo, it was clear that nine days was time to scratch only the surface. Undaunted by the weather, our Squadron Chaplain, "Wild Bill" Wilcox, led a hardy band in the rain, on a two-day climb of Mount Fujiyama.

With not one but two completely rebricked boilers and every unofficial nook and cranny of the ship stuffed with souvenirs, cases of china, and even a motorcycle, we departed into the teeth of Tropical Storm Trixie. In company and under our tactical command was USS *Weiss* (APD-135), a destroyer escort converted to high-speed transport of troops. Despite the 20-30 foot seas on the first night out, we managed to conduct considerable training enroute. An overnight stop for fuel at Buckner Bay, Okinawa, gave about 90 men an opportunity to tour some of the Ryukuan villages near the base, and then it was hustle all the way to Subic, staying one day ahead of Typhoon Wendy, and just behind Tropical Storm Bess.

Following two days providing gunfire support training for marine spotters, we set course for Tonkin to begin our last tour on the line: Three intensive weeks which schedules *Steinaker* for a variety of missions including Operation "Sea Dragon" and the gunline.

26 September 1968

Excerpts From The Captain's Log #11

Subic to "Sea Dragon" to Yankee Station

ENROUTE TO "SEA DRAGON" Operations we exercised the ASW team, firing exercise torpedoes from our tube mounts and from our DASH. This would ordinarily be very exciting, however the anticipation of participating in the most challenging destroyer assignment in the Seventh Fleet made us impatient. We felt quite confident. We had had a successful tour on the gunline; the crew had performed magnificently when taken under accurate fire by enemy shore batteries in July, and we were prepared. The press releases speak for themselves. The days flew by; the quick orientation to a new job, the high speed runs in toward the beach, firing suppression missions against coastal defense sites while the longer gunned ship, the heavy cruiser *Boston*, fired a

Front Row L to R
Donahue PN1
Adams SN
Stueber YN2
Fay HMC

Back Row L to R
Conroy LTJG
Clark YNSN
Pierotti SN
Zalesny SN

planned interdiction mission coordinated with bombing attacks by Navy carrier-based strike aircraft. This, followed by a high-speed retirement to minimize our exposure to hostile fire, was pretty heady stuff, as the Captain kept hearing in the back of his mind – the off-the-record order – "Captain, get the job done – but don't get hit. Don't sacrifice your sailors."

It was all over much too quickly and then it was back to Yankee Station.

SOME OF OUR PRESS CLIPPINGS follow, and I am appending a lengthier piece by Seventh Fleet journalist, PHC A. L. Smith, USN

On Board USS *Steinaker* (DD-863) in the Gulf of Tonkin 12 September 1968

"It took five months and two weeks for us to make it from Norfolk to Operation Sea Dragon, but we're here now and I think the North Vietnamese know it," commented Chief Gunner's Mate Von Banks, after this Seventh Fleet Destroyer fired on and damaged a large North Vietnamese logistics craft during her first day of firing off the coast of North Vietnam. Banks, who was recently awarded the Navy Unit Commendation Medal for service a board the nuclear attack aircraft carrier, USS *Enterprise* (CVA(N)-65) on a previous tour of duty in the Gulf of Tonkin in support of Allied Forces ashore, is responsible for supervising the maintenance and operation of *Steinaker*'s two 5-inch gun mounts. "It's a lot different in a destroyer," says Banks. "Here our guns are our reason for being. On a carrier they are just a side attraction."

On watch during the attack, Second Class Sonarman Ronald

L. Balcom of Independence, Missouri said, "the target was too far away for us to pick it up on sonar, but our shots came through loud and clear."

On Board USS *Steinaker* (DD-863) 12 September 1968

During a relatively quiet day off the coast of North Vietnam, this Norfolk-based destroyer fired two missions in company with USS *Berkeley* (DDG-15). "It's hard to tell what we're doing from my station in after steering," said Seaman Rudolph Bischoff of Richmond, Virginia. "I know which way we are headed and when the guns go off and that's about it until the mission's over and I can come back topside."

In addition to two firing missions, today also brought two new sons to Bischoff, whose wife, Ann Carol's delivery of twins was the big news of the day aboard *Steinaker*.

On station in *Steinaker*'s Combat Information Center, Radarman Third Class Barry McCauley of Bridgeport, West Virginia was in a much better position to know what was going on. "Things went much smoother today," *Steinaker*'s second day of a new assignment off North Vietnam. "No matter how much training we do, it's never quite like the real thing, even though we did the same sort of operation near Phan Thiet in July and August." McCauley and others remember the 24-hour non-stop exercises the previous winter at Bloodsworth Island, Virginia. Had we not qualified at gunfire support we would not have been permitted on this operation. "We were exhausted but the skipper made us give it one more try, and we finished just before the midnight deadline," he added.

For *Steinaker*'s engineers, life during shore bombardment is pretty much like life underway anywhere else, and they, like

First Row: Conte; Dolhmar; Bolton; Dickerson; Baum-gardner; Orson 2nd; Rushing; Radley; Jenkens; Grant; Cherry; Vernon; Yoho; Thomas Btc. 3rd; Dowell; Ost-land; Staples; Connor; Kukla; Vincent Last; Tucker; Cheeks; Lindaman; Corpal; Lloyd; Burks

seaman Bischoff, must usually wait until after a mission to find out how effectively the ship prosecuted its assigned targets.

Fireman Chuck Minnett of Warren, Ohio says, "the only real difference is that it takes longer for me to make my rounds as Soundings and Security Patrol. I have to check the same spaces but because of the higher condition of readiness and the number of hatches closed between compartments, I have to move fast to get around the entire ship each hour."

On Board USS *Steinaker* (DD-863) 14 September 1968

Yesterday was certainly a Friday the thirteenth for two waterborne logistics craft beached near Mui Ron Ca, sixty miles North of the Demilitarized Zone (DMZ). Working in company with USS *Berkeley* (DDG-15), *Steinaker* opened fire near sunset, damaging both North Vietnamese vessels.

In order to avoid possible shore fire from known coastal defense sites, this Norfolk-based destroyer opened fire at long range. Fire Control Director Officer, Chief Sonarman Raymond A. Stewart of Parkersburg, West Virginia, commented, "We've never fired at that great a range before. It's normally beyond the critical maximum range of our guns. Our first rounds landed only 50 yards off target, however. That would be good shooting at half the range. And using proximity ammunition, normally used only for anti-aircraft firing, resulted in airburst just above the vessels, effectively shattering them from stem to stern."

6 October 1968

Excerpts From The Captain's Log #12

Yankee Station to Gunline to Subic to Guam

THE LAST TOUR on Yankee Station was blessedly brief and we joined the other ships of DESDIV 21 for our final week of combat operations. Our mission: Support of the U.S. First Field Force in Vietnam. It was an interesting period, as we divided our efforts between the harassment and interdiction of enemy movements in the vicinity of Tuy Hoa (this mostly at night), and the support of amphibious assault operations 30 miles north, near Qui Nhon. I couldn't help reflecting that it was the vicious destruction of a bachelor enlisted quarters in Qui Nhon, resulting in the death of many U.S. servicemen in early February 1965, which was the direct cause of the first air attack on North Vietnam. The highlight of this last tour on the gunline was a tremendous bombardment, by *Steinaker*, which lasted over four hours and which paved the way for a highly successful landing and sweep operation by Coastal Group 22. On 1 October we trained our guns centerline, secured our mount crews, and headed for Subic Bay, for a frenetic logistics turnaround, following which we sailed at dusk, formed our proud column, and began the long voyage home via the San Bernardino Straits (scene of a famous WWII naval engagement) to Guam.

The following was received from Commander Cruiser-Destroyer Group Seventh Fleet:

FAREWELL. As you depart the Cruiser-Destroyer Group, Seventh Fleet, you can be justifiably proud of the contribution you have made in every area of destroyer employment. The high tempo of operations never discouraged nor impeded your ability to accomplish your missions. To the officers and men of *Blandy, Borie, Steinaker,* and *Rich,* I extend my personal thanks for the services rendered and my best wishes for continued success in the future. Rear Admiral Moore.

22 October 1968

To the *Steinaker* Family and Friends,

FINALLY THE RUDDER has been shifted and the ship steadied on a course for home. It was with a sigh of relief that the final round of our deployment was fired, signaling, as in a football game, the end of the physical effort. We departed the gunline on 1 October and after refueling and reprovisioning in Subic Bay, joined up with the other ships of our division to commence the long voyage to Norfolk.

With the exception of Operation Sea Dragon, our last tour in the combat zone found *Steinaker* performing tasks similar to those she had been called upon to perform in previous tours. Again, we participated in anti-submarine training exercises in order to retain our readiness in this area. And again, we were assigned escort destroyer duties, this time for the attack carrier USS *Constellation* (CVA-64). We also provided naval gunfire support to U.S. and South Vietnamese forces ashore in an area South of Danang, not too far from our earlier assignment in late July.

Sea Dragon is an assignment that most destroyer crews look forward to with great anticipation and excitement. It's a risky business and the ship is constantly under the threat of being fired upon by enemy gun emplacements. For this reason, more than any other, each man is required to put forth his best effort, and be continually alert. As a unit of the Northern Sea Dragon organization, *Steinaker* carried out 22 pre-planned missions against coastal defense sites along the North Vietnamese coastline. Our primary mission was to interdict and destroy waterborne logistics craft engaged in the transport of war materiéls to Viet Cong forces in the South. Our task unit accounted for the destruction of 12 of these craft and damage to 14 others during the one week of our assignment alone.

Now that the deployment is over, except for the transit home, I feel sincerely grateful and extremely fortunate that *Steinaker* was capable of accomplishing her mission successfully and of making a direct and significant contribution to our country's effort in Vietnam with no material casualties and, most importantly, no serious personnel injuries. Surely all your prayers for our safe return home have been answered, and I hope that very shortly it will be possible for you to be reunited with your sons and husbands for an enjoyable leave period.

By the time of our arrival in Norfolk, we will have been deployed for 224 days. Of this time, 185 days, or 83% of our time, has been at sea, nearly 50% of this in the combat zone. We will have steamed nearly 60,000 miles, consumed 24,218 pounds of potatoes and 16.8 tons of meat. It has been quite a deployment by any standard.

Some of you, I know, are delighted with the recent directive issued by the Secretary of the Navy which will terminate the service of our two-year obligated reserve personnel sooner than expected. It is with a certain amount of regret, however, that we who stay on will witness the loss of these fine men shortly after our return to Norfolk, many of whom are making such excellent progress towards advancement to petty officer status. For those of you who made the personal sacrifice associated with your husband or son's extension of active duty to complete this cruise, I am truly grateful. Without their experience and ability the fine record attained by *Steinaker* during this deployment would never have been possible.

Sincerely,

H. H. Sacks, Commanding

P.S. For your information, I am enclosing a copy of the official summary of *Steinaker*'s operations.

31 October 1968

Excerpts From The Captain's Log #14

Guam to Midway to Pearl Harbor to San Diego to Panama

THERE IS NO END to training; first we train for war, and this is really the easiest kind of training – well motivated, understandable. Now we train for a period of somewhat lessened readiness, knowing

First Row: Chief Wall, Woolvine, Leary, Lang, Yinger, McAdams, Duvlea, Chief Mayes Second Row: Bozek, Mathis, Smith, Baur, Conroy, Diehl, Hallenbeck, Blum- oefer, Wagner Third Row: Snyder, Miller, McFarland, Boteler, Kapitan, Donnell

that return from a major deployment always means a step-down in available personnel to handle emergency situations. Some on leave, some at schools, some transferred ashore to be replaced by the less experienced, and some to be released from active duty without replacement; thus our trip home, far from being a dull one, has been full of training – training for those days ahead when *Steinaker* is not steaming proudly with her full war complement, ready to deal with anything a destroyer might face.

Just as we took comfort during our transit out to WESTPAC in the ship's successful full power trials, our engineers rightfully walk with their heads high, as we again conducted a complete full power trail, this time between Pearl Harbor and San Diego, and after seven months and 47,000 miles of fast-paced operations, the plant performed better and with greater efficiency than on the way out.

Transits home are generally agonizingly slow; ours has been very busy, as we received our annual Administrative Inspection enroute, culminating in a personnel inspection given by our Commodore, Captain Dunham. It was one of those truly beautiful and rare moments in any skipper's tour. This crew, intensely proud of its achievement and deeply saddened by the inevitable breakup of the team, and understanding that this was the last time they would stand together before an inspection party, this crew was a knockout. I was touched, because I realized that no amount of hounding or persuasion could get each and every man turned out with such perfection. This was something they wanted for themselves, and it was worth it. "I have been involved in both ends of inspections for thirty years, giving them and getting them, and this is the finest looking crew I have ever seen. Your outstanding appearance attests to your professional pride in your performance." That was the Commodore speaking to all hands. The Captain could only agree.

I am attaching a brief summary of *Steinaker*'s tour with the Seventh Fleet. You might call it the "official history." We rejoin the Atlantic Fleet today and begin our last leg home. We are a little tired. We are more than a little homesick. I am grateful for

First Row: Hallenbeck MMC, Guest DC1, Anderson SF1, Clark, Gundy, Hagemeyer, ENS Rouse   Second Row: Minney, Bednar, Oliver, Harrison, Benheighm   Back Row: Seifert, Pittman

the privilege of taking this fine ship into combat, thankful for the good fortune in bringing her safely home, but most of all, very, very proud to have been the Captain of this crew.

Summary of Operations

USS *Steinaker* (DD-863) 20 May 1968-1 Oct. 1968

DURING THE PERIOD 20 May through 1 October, USS *Steinaker* was assigned to the U.S. Seventh Fleet and participated in naval gunfire support operations in Binh Thuan and Phu Yen Provinces, Sea Dragon operations off the coast of North Viet Nam in the vicinity of Mui Ron, anti-air warfare picket duties off the Demilitarized Zone (DMZ) and acted as escort destroyer for five different attack carriers during an intense period of air strike operations against strategic targets located in North Vietnam.

While supporting the 3rd Battalion, 506th Infantry, 101st Airborne Division and ARVN Regional Forces in the execution of Operation McLain, an allied thrust against Viet Cong infiltration in South Vietnam, *Steinaker*'s gunfire continually preceded friendly force movement and minimized enemy troop build-up and concentration. Her accurate firepower was provided consistently for forces ashore and was used without hesitation in the close support of friendly troops.

During the period 2-6 July 1968, the Commanding Officer, USS *Steinaker* (DD-863) assumed duty as CTU 77.0.4, an anti-air warfare picket unit, providing early warning against possible enemy airborne intrusion from the vicinity of the DMZ.

During this period, a U.S. airborne vehicle was recovered from the Gulf of Tonkin. This recovery was considered to be a significant contribution to the United States' intelligence effort in Vietnam.

On 6 July, while operating in the vicinity of the DMZ, *Steinaker* received fire from a hostile gun emplacement located on Tigre Island. The ship received 25 rounds, some less than 15 yards away, and was bracketed several times during the engagement, in which *Steinaker*'s almost simultaneous counter-battery fire silenced and possibly destroyed the gun emplacement according to an airborne spotting unit which entered the area to provide support to *Steinaker*. This rapid reaction permitted the ship to retire unscathed at the same time causing damage to the enemy.

In mid-September, *Steinaker* operated as a unit of TU 77.1.1 Northern Sea Dragon, and in this capacity carried out 22 preplanned missions against coastal defense sites along the North Vietnamese coastline. The primary mission of this task unit was the interdiction and destruction of waterborne logistics craft engaged in the transport of war supplies to the South and to provide naval gunfire against targets of opportunity spotted by carrier based aircraft. *Steinaker* suppressed 20 coastal defense sites while the longer-range 5-inch/54-caliber gun equipped ships fired on strategic targets located farther inland. The efforts of the task unit accounted for destruction of 12 waterborne logistics craft and damage to 14 others.

From 26 September to 1 October, *Steinaker* provided gunfire support to friendly forces ashore. Harassment and interdiction fire was effective in minimizing enemy troop activities along the coast of Phu Yen Province during a period in which intelligence revealed plans for an enemy build-up in this area. On 28 September and again on 30 September, pre-assault gunfire was provided for two amphibious landings designed to sweep areas of known Viet Cong activity. In both missions, *Steinaker*'s effective and accurate gunfire, which resulted in a total of eight bunkers

Left to Right Last Row: Morton, SN, Gales, SN, Carter, SN, Maxwell, SN, James, SN, Beach, SK3 Third Row: Marrow, SN, Lake, SN, Varnes, CS1, Getter, SN, Patrick, SK1, Meyer, SN Second Row: Lee, SN, Lacanlale, TN, Brooks, SN, Labbadia, CS3, Barredo, DK1, Lauderman, SN, Brown, SK1, McGrath, SN Front Row: Horsch, LTJG, Juan, TN, Kestner, SN, Jones, CS3, Gonzales, SD2, Fiely, SK3, Fiely, SH3, Taylor, SH2, Souther, CSC

destroyed, two damaged, one sampan destroyed, and one Viet Cong structure destroyed, enabled the landings to take place completely unopposed and with no casualties to assault forces. Sweeping U.S. and SVN forces discovered positive evidence of enemy movements in an area threatening a major U.S. installation.

The USS *Steinaker*, in fulfilling every commitment, meeting every rendezvous as assigned, and completing every task, successfully maintained her material readiness in a manner second to no other destroyer in the Seventh Fleet, suffering no major casualty during the entire deployment, either in engineering, electronics, or weapons systems. *Steinaker*'s high state of combat readiness throughout the deployment was further reflected by the fact that not one serious personnel injury was sustained by the crew despite the most rigorous operating conditions which included 55 underway replenishments, over 150 helo transfers, 17 helo in flight refuelings during day and night conditions, and over 30 evolutions involving the use of small boats.

★

ABOUT THE AUTHOR

COMMANDER Harold H. (Hal) Sacks was born in New York City in 1930. A graduate of Syracuse University (BA) and Columbia University (MA), Hal served as a naval officer from 1952 to 1972, earning the Bronze Star Medal with Combat V,

 the Meritorious Service Medal, the Joint Service Commendation Medal, the Vietnamese Cross of Gallantry, the Korean Presidential Unit Citation, and the Combat Action Medal, along with numerous service medals.

From 1972 until 2005 he enjoyed careers in business and fundraising for non-profit organizations. He has been a frequent contributor to the *U.S. Naval Institute Proceedings*, and has been the book review editor for the *Southeastern Virginia Jewish News* for thirty years.

He and his wife, the former Annabel Lee Glicksman, have two children, five grandchildren and one great-grandson.

CPSIA information can be obtained at www.ICGtesting.com
Printed in the USA
BVOW08*0104211113

336885BV00003B/313/P